UNDERSTANDING THE HOLOCAUST

Holocaust Camps and Killing Centers

Craig E. Blohm

ReferencePoint
Press®

San Diego, CA

About the Author

Craig E. Blohm has written numerous books and magazine articles for young readers. He and his wife, Desiree, reside in Tinley Park, Illinois.

© 2016 ReferencePoint Press, Inc.
Printed in the United States

For more information, contact:
ReferencePoint Press, Inc.
PO Box 27779
San Diego, CA 92198
www.ReferencePointPress.com

LIBRARY OF CONGRESS CATALOGING-IN-PUBLICATION DATA

Blohm, Craig E., 1948- author.
  Holocaust camps and killing centers / by Craig E. Blohm.
    pages cm. -- (Understanding the Holocaust series)
  Includes bibliographical references and index.
  ISBN-13: 978-1-60152-842-1 (hardback)
  ISBN-10: 1-60152-842-6 (hardback)
  1. World War, 1939-1945--Concentration camps--Juvenile literature. 2. Holocaust, Jewish (1939-1945)--Juvenile literature. I. Title.
  D805.A2B64 2016
  940.53'185--dc23
                                                                        2014043333

CONTENTS

1941
Germany invades the Soviet Union; the Germans massacre about one hundred thousand Jews, Roma (Gypsies), Communists, and others at Babi Yar in Ukraine; the United States declares war on Japan and Germany after Japan attacks Pearl Harbor.

1937
Buchenwald concentration camp is established in east-central Germany.

1920
The Nazi Party publishes its 25-point program declaring its intention to segregate Jews from so-called Aryan society and to eliminate the political, legal, and civil rights of Germany's Jewish population.

1925
Adolf Hitler's autobiographical manifesto *Mein Kampf* is published; in it he outlines his political ideology and future plans for Germany and calls for the violent elimination of the world's Jews.

1940
The Warsaw ghetto—a 1.3 square mile (3.4 sq km) area sealed off from the rest of the city by high walls, barbed wire, and armed guards—is established in Poland.

1920 / 1934 1936 1938 1940

1918
The Treaty of Versailles, marking the formal end of World War I and a humiliating defeat for Germany, is signed.

1935
The Nuremberg Laws, excluding German Jews from citizenship and depriving them of the right to vote and hold public office, are enacted.

1939
Germany invades Poland, igniting World War II in Europe; in Warsaw, Jews are forced to wear white armbands with a blue Star of David.

1933
Hitler is appointed Germany's chancellor; the Gestapo is formed; Dachau concentration camp is established.

1938
Violent anti-Jewish attacks known as *Kristallnacht* (Night of Broken Glass) take place throughout greater Germany; the first *Kindertransport* (children's transport) arrives in Great Britain with thousands of Jewish children seeking refuge from Nazi persecution.

1942
The Nazi plan to annihilate Europe's Jews (the Final Solution) is outlined at the Wannsee Conference in Berlin; deportations of about 1.5 million Jews to killing centers in Poland begin.

1944
Allied forces carry out the D-Day invasion at Normandy in France; diplomats in Budapest offer protection to Jews.

1946
The International Military Tribunal imposes death and prison sentences during the Nuremberg Trials.

1948
The State of Israel is established as a homeland for the world's Jews.

1949
Argentina grants asylum to Josef Mengele, the notorious SS doctor who performed medical experiments on prisoners in Auschwitz.

1942   **1944**   **1946**   **1948** / **1970**

1943
Despite armed Jewish resistance, the Nazis move to liquidate ghettos in Poland and the Soviet Union; Denmark actively resists Nazi attempts to deport its Jewish citizens.

1960
In Argentina, Israeli intelligence agents abduct Adolf Eichmann, one of the masterminds of the Holocaust; he is brought to Israel to stand trial for crimes against the Jewish people.

1945
Allied forces liberate Auschwitz, Buchenwald, and Dachau concentration camps; Hitler commits suicide; World War II ends with the surrender of Germany and Japan; the Nuremberg Trials begin with war crimes indictments against leading Nazis.

1981
More than ten thousand survivors attend the first World Gathering of Jewish Holocaust Survivors in Israel; a similar gathering two years later in Washington, DC, attracts twenty thousand people.

1947
The UN General Assembly adopts a resolution partitioning Palestine into Jewish and Arab states; Holocaust survivor Simon Wiesenthal opens a center in Austria to search for Nazis who have evaded justice.

The Camps of the Third Reich

The year 1933 was a turning point in the history of Germany. Adolf Hitler, leader of the National Socialist German Workers' Party, commonly known as the Nazi Party, was appointed the nation's chancellor. Having gained his position using intimidation and violence, Hitler was ruthless toward all who opposed his regime, the Third *Reich* (Third Empire). He was especially suspicious of Communists, whom he accused of planning to overthrow the government. He also blamed them for a devastating fire that gutted the *Reichstag* (parliament) building. To isolate and control his political opponents Hitler ordered the construction of the first of what would become a vast system of concentration camps throughout Europe.

The First Camp

As Hitler's power grew, more and more of his political opponents were rounded up and sent to prison. Soon German prisons could no longer handle the ever increasing flow of inmates, so local police authorities erected detention centers. These were makeshift camps that confined prisoners in warehouses, abandoned military barracks, old castles, or anywhere else that large groups of people could be detained. Before long it became apparent that even these camps could not deal with the mounting inmate population. A more permanent and systematic solution was needed.

Dachau, the first true Nazi concentration camp (*Konzentrationslager*), was located near the Bavarian town of the same name. In a press release German police chief and commander of the SS (*Schutzstaffel* or "protection squadron") Heinrich Himmler announced, "On Wednesday [March 22, 1933] the first concentration camp will be opened near Dachau. It has a capacity of 5,000 persons. Here all the Communist and—as far as necessary—Reichsbanner [a Nazi opposition group] and Marxist functionaries who threaten the security of the state will be concentrated."[1] Established in an abandoned munitions factory, Dachau began operation with about two hundred inmates relocated from German prisons. By the end of 1933 about forty-eight hundred political prisoners were interned at the camp without trial or explanation. As the original concentration camp, Dachau became the model for the camps that would be constructed throughout Nazi Germany and the territories it conquered at the beginning of World War II. It was also the training ground for the Nazis who would become administrators and guards of future concentration camps.

Expanding the System

More than twenty thousand camps of various sizes were eventually constructed. This network stretched from France in the west to Ukraine in the east and from Norway in the north to as far south as Greece. As the system expanded, different types of camps were created for specific purposes. Concentration camps such as Buchenwald, Bergen-Belsen, and Sachsenhausen removed from society people thought to represent a danger to the Third Reich—or, in the language of the Nazis, "undesirables." These included Communists, criminals, homosexuals, Roma and Sinti (Gypsies), and Jews. Another type of facility called the transit camp was established mainly in the occupied western European countries of France, Belgium, Luxembourg, and the Netherlands. Mechelen in Belgium, Amersfoort and Westerbork in the Netherlands, Drancy in France, and other transit camps were temporary collection points for holding prisoners before sending them to other camps. Sometimes they were sent to labor camps such as Mauthausen, Mittelbau-Dora, and Ravensbrück—all located in Nazi-occupied Poland. Labor camp prisoners worked at jobs ranging from constructing roads, bridges, and buildings in the Reich to making uniforms and weapons for the German army.

Prisoners lived in squalid conditions in all of these camps. They often had to wait hours to get watered-down soup, moldy bread, and rancid coffee—a daily ration of food that provided little nutrition. Their civilian clothes were confiscated and replaced with thin striped prison uniforms that offered no protection from the winter cold.

Savagely burned alive by SS troops in April 1945, a concentration camp prisoner rests in a gruesome pose of death. The Nazis created a vast system of camps intended to further their goals of conquering Europe and annihilating Europe's Jews.

Medical treatment was virtually nonexistent, and death from disease, starvation, and exposure was common. Those who disobeyed the orders of their guards or tried to escape were immediately shot.

A fourth type of camp, the extermination camp or killing center, was added to carry out Hitler's "Final Solution to the Jewish Question." As a young man, Hitler viewed Jews as *Untermenschen*, or less than human. His anti-Semitism, or hatred of Jews, deepened after Germany lost World War I, a defeat Hitler blamed partly on German Jews. In 1933 about 9.5 million Jews, or about 60 percent of the world's Jewish population, lived in Europe. With his newly acquired power, Hitler could now act on his anti-Semitic prejudices. In a speech to the Reichstag, he proclaimed, "If the international Jewish financiers in and outside Europe should succeed in plunging nations once more into a world war, then the result will [be] . . . the annihilation of the Jewish race in Europe."[2]

Six killing centers—Auschwitz, Belzec, Chelmno, Majdanek, Sobibor, and Treblinka—were established between 1940 and 1942 in occupied Poland. They existed for only one purpose: the extermination of Jews. Every day, crowded trains pulled into the camps bearing internees from the transit camps or from Jewish urban districts called ghettos. Those who survived the journey were eventually poisoned in gas chambers; cremation ovens operating twenty-four hours a day disposed of the remains of the dead. By the time World War II ended in 1945, some 11 million people, including almost 6 million Jews, had been murdered by the Nazis.

> "If the international Jewish financiers in and outside Europe should succeed in plunging nations once more into a world war, then the result will [be] . . . the annihilation of the Jewish race in Europe."[2]
>
> —Adolf Hitler, Chancellor of Germany.

Legacy of the Camps

The knowledge of the evils committed during the Holocaust in Hitler's camps and killing centers still evokes feelings of horror. Relatively few prisoners survived their time in the camps. The Registry of Holocaust Survivors at the United States Holocaust Memorial Museum lists some two hundred thousand names of those who survived internment or persecution by the Nazis. Many have shared their stories in books, in radio and television interviews, and on film. Their hope is that those who met their fates in the gas chambers and ovens of the Holocaust camps will not be forgotten.

CHAPTER ONE

Journey to Extinction

On September 1, 1939, German troops invaded Poland, beginning World War II. On that day Chaim A. Kaplan, a Jewish scholar and educator living in the Polish capital of Warsaw, wrote in his diary, "We are witnessing the dawn of a new era in the history of the world. This war will indeed bring destruction upon human civilization."[3] Of the 35 million people living in Poland, about 3.5 million, or 10 percent of the population, were Jews. For them, and for the rest of the Jews of Eastern Europe, the destruction that Kaplan predicted would be accomplished by the worst act of genocide in history.

For thousands of years Jews had been viewed as being dishonest, peculiar, and untrustworthy. As early as the thirteenth century, European Jews were forced to live separate from the general society in urban districts called ghettos. Within these walled areas Jews struggled daily with crowded and unsanitary living conditions. The gates of the ghettos could be closed from the inside in times of the persecution of Jews, and from the outside during Christian holidays from which Jews were banned. By the nineteenth century, Jews had become fully integrated into European society, and most of the ghettos had vanished. But under Hitler's Third Reich, ghettos returned as a means to once more limit the freedom of the Jews.

Jews Forced into Ghettos

The first step in the journey toward near extinction for Poland's Jews was the establishment of ghettos. The Jews were to be forcibly relocated from their homes in cities throughout Poland (and eventually the rest of Europe) and isolated in these walled and guarded communities. The responsibility for implementation of this plan fell to SS *Obergruppenführer* (Lieutenant General) Reinhard Heydrich, the head of the Reich Main Security Office. In a conference held on January 20, 1942, in the Berlin suburb of Wannsee, Heydrich laid out the plan for the heads of various government agencies.

The first prerequisite for the final aim is the concentration of the Jews from the countryside into the larger cities. This is to be carried out with all speed. . . . As few concentration points as possible are to be set up, so as to facilitate subsequent measures. In this connection, it is to be borne in mind that only cities that are rail junctions, or at least located along railroad lines, are to be designated as concentration points.[4]

Heydrich's use of the phrases "final aim" and "subsequent measures" was his way of conveying the goal of exterminating Jews without explicitly admitting the Reich's plans for mass murder. Many high-ranking Nazis, including Hitler himself, used such neutral words to obscure the true nature of the Final Solution. In this way they hoped to avoid being held accountable for their murderous acts should Germany lose the war. Adolf Eichmann, a lieutenant colonel in the SS, was assigned to handle the details of deporting Jews to the ghettos and later to the concentration camps.

Jews were not only transported from the ghettos in Poland but from all over German-occupied territory in Europe, including France, Belgium, the Netherlands, Austria, Czechoslovakia, Yugoslavia, and Greece. Approximately one thousand ghettos were established in the General Government region of occupied Poland. The first ghetto was built in the Polish city of Piotrkow Trybunalski on October 8, 1939. As many as twenty-eight thousand Jews were crowded into a section of the city where only six thousand people had previously resided. Conditions were miserable, as nine-year-old survivor Hanka Ziegler later recalled: "We all stayed in one little room, the seven of us. Another 14 people came to the room at different times. . . . My father got caught foraging for food and was put in prison. I never saw my father again."[5] The Warsaw ghetto, the largest in the General Government region, was created to segregate nearly a half million Jews behind a brick wall 8 feet (2.4 m) high. The Jews themselves were forced to pay the construction costs of the wall. Life

> "We are witnessing the dawn of a new era in the history of the world. This war will indeed bring destruction upon human civilization."[3]
>
> —Jewish scholar Chaim Kaplan.

Nazi police inspect the documents of Jews forced to live in the Warsaw ghetto in Poland. Life in the ghettos was a daily struggle; thousands died of starvation and disease.

in the Warsaw ghetto was a daily struggle; thousands died of starvation and disease.

Ghetto inhabitants were forbidden to leave their walled enclaves and were forced to wear a yellow Star of David identifying them as Jews. The Nazis fully expected—and hoped—that many Jews would die in the ghettos. In an official report Hans Frank, the Governor-General of the region, states, "It is not necessary to dwell on the fact that we are sentencing the Jews to death. If the Jews do not die of starvation, it will be necessary to step up anti-Jewish measures, and let us hope that, too, will come to pass."[6]

With tens of thousands of Jews imprisoned in the ghettos, the Nazis prepared for the next stage of Hitler's Final Solution: deportation to concentration camps throughout Europe. A key element in this process was the German national system of railroads, the *Deutsche Reichsbahn*.

Deportation

The Holocaust could not have happened without the use of Germany's railroads. So extensive was the *Reichsbahn* that it took 1.4 million workers to keep the trains scheduled and running efficiently. During World War II the railroads transported troops, war materiel, and other essential goods throughout Germany and the occupied territories. Beginning in 1941 the trains were pressed into service to transport Jews from the ghettos to their final destination: the camps and killing centers.

The order usually came unexpectedly. Ghetto dwellers were instructed to gather their possessions and assemble at a central location: a school, a meeting hall, or the town square. They followed orders, for to disobey meant death. But their ultimate fate was never truthfully revealed. They were told that they were being resettled to labor camps in the east. Promises of more food and better living conditions waiting at the end of the line gave many a false sense of hope. Still, many Jews were apprehensive about the journey. Although life in the ghettos was miserable, it was familiar. Resettlement was an unknown, and the Jews feared they might be separated from their families, perhaps never to be reunited. But when the order was given, the assembled Jews were marched through the streets of the ghetto to the trains that waited to take them to the camps.

> "It is not necessary to dwell on the fact that we are sentencing the Jews to death. If the Jews do not die of starvation, it will be necessary to step up anti-Jewish measures, and let us hope that, too, will come to pass."[6]
>
> —Governor-general of Nazi-occupied Polish territory.

Conditions on the Trains

The deportees did not ride in comfortable passenger cars but were jammed into freight and cattle cars for a trip that could last days or weeks. From 80 to 140 people were packed into each car, forced to stand or, if there was room, sit on the floor. The cars were sealed tight, with only small cracks in the wooden sides or floor for air to circulate. Once the doors were slammed shut, ventilation was almost nonexistent, and many deportees fought for a place to stand near a crack just

The Engineer of Death

Transporting Jews to the ghettos and camps during the Holocaust was a massive and complicated job that fell to Adolf Eichmann. Born in Solingen, Germany, in 1906, Eichmann joined the Nazi Party at age twenty-six, ultimately becoming a lieutenant colonel in the SS. He became the Nazi's "Jewish expert" while working in the "Jewish Section" of the SS intelligence agency, the *Sicherheitsdienst*. In 1938 he simplified the process of emigration for Jews who wished to voluntarily leave the Reich. To achieve the goal of a "Jew-free" Germany, Eichmann stepped up his activities. By 1942 he was coordinating the forced deportation of thousands of Jews from the ghettos to the death camps. Eichmann handled the job with his usual skilled efficiency.

After the war Eichmann was captured by the Allies but escaped and went into hiding in Argentina. Recaptured in 1960 by an Israeli intelligence team, Eichmann was tried and convicted of war crimes. He was hanged in 1962. Although he professed his innocence during the trial, a statement Eichmann made in 1945 reveals his true nature: "I will leap into my grave laughing because the feeling that I have five million human beings on my conscience is for me a source of extraordinary satisfaction."

Quoted in *Jewish Currents*, "December 11: Eichmann Trial." http://jewishcurrents.org.

to get a bit of fresh air. The stench in the cars was horrible. Sanitation consisted of a bucket for human waste, which was difficult and embarrassing to use. Many passengers had no choice but to soil themselves when the need for relief became too great.

Most trains carried between one thousand to two thousand deportees, although some held five thousand or more. The heavily overloaded trains could travel at only about 30 miles per hour (48.3 km/h), lengthening the trip and prolonging the agony of those jammed into the cars. It was not unusual for a train to be routed onto a spur track and left standing for days while higher priority trains carrying war supplies were allowed through on the main line. Primo Levi, an author and survivor of the Holocaust, recalls his five-day train ride to the Auschwitz killing center:

> We suffered from thirst and cold: at every stop we clamored for water, or even a handful of snow, but we were rarely heard. The soldiers of the escort drove off anybody who tried to approach the convoy. Two young mothers, nursing their children, groaned night and day, begging for water. Our state

Ghettos, Camps, and Killing Centers, 1942

Extermination camp
Concentration camp*
City with a ghetto
Major massacre
Axis country or country annexed by the Axis
Occupied by Axis
Allied country
Neutral country
*Includes labor, prison, and transit camps

Note: dotted lines show present-day borders

of nervous tension made the hunger, exhaustion, and lack of sleep seem less of a torment. But the hours of darkness were nightmares without end.[7]

Sweltering in the summer and freezing in the winter, many people on the trains died before reaching the end of the line. Suffocation, exposure to the elements, suicide, and even vicious attacks by desperate fellow deportees killed numerous passengers. SS officer Kurt Gerstein witnessed a train arriving at a camp carrying "45 wagons [freight cars] with 6,700 people of whom 1,450 were already dead on arrival."[8] Rena Kornreich Gelissen, then a twenty-one-year-old passenger, recalls, "Somebody dies. We try to move away from the corpse, there's no place to go. I have never been so close to death."[9] There was no time to pay proper Jewish respect for the deceased. At some point a train was stopped, the doors briefly opened by guards shouting orders. Gelissen describes such a scene:

> "Somebody dies. We try to move away from the corpse, there's no place to go. I have never been so close to death."[9]
>
> —Holocaust train passenger Rena Kornreich Gelissen.

> "Throw out your dead!" The orders are immune to our pain. Bodies are tossed out as unceremoniously as the bucket, which is also dumped. The door slams shut too quickly, severing the outside world from our senses. Now that we have something to compare it to, the closeness is more suffocating than before. The train continues its endless trek.[10]

The few meager possessions the Jews were allowed to bring with them, especially valuables like money and jewelry, were often stolen by the guards. On one train a guard demanded thirty wristwatches from the passengers. If he did not get them, he declared, he would kill everyone in the car. The watches were provided, and the guard returned to his post. Ada Lichtman recalls that on her train, "Soldiers entered the car and robbed us and even cut off fingers with rings. They claimed that we didn't need them any more."[11] Many of the guards were constantly drunk, a condition that only intensified their cruelty toward the deportees. Sometimes drunk guards fired their machine guns into the locked freight cars merely for sport.

After days of suffering, the deported Jews finally arrived at their destination. For most, hope ran high that this new location would be an improvement over the ghettos. After all, the Nazis had promised that they would have work to occupy them, good food to nourish them, and improved living conditions. All too soon they discovered that the Nazis had lied about the life, and death, that awaited them.

Arrival

As the trains pulled into the camp stations SS guards were waiting on the platform. "We were alerted by the sound of the soldiers' boots as

On arrival at Auschwitz in 1939, Jews line up for the selection process that will determine who lives and who dies. Disoriented from the difficult journey, newly arrived deportees were often greeted by uniformed SS guards shouting orders or shooting people where they stood.

An Island for the Jews

In the early 1940s many ideas were advanced for solving the "Jewish Question." One unusual plan called for relocating all European Jews to their own island.

By 1940 it had become apparent that the General Government region could not hold all the Jewish deportees the Nazis intended to send there. So they revived a plan that had been discussed by anti-Semites since the nineteenth century: The Jews would be rounded up and shipped to Madagascar, a French island in the Indian Ocean off the eastern coast of Africa. Under the Madagascar Plan, the French inhabitants of the island would be displaced by some 4 million Jews. In effect, the island would become one huge Jewish ghetto. After Germany's defeat of France, Hitler himself approved the plan.

While the idea may have been appealing to the Nazis, it was hardly feasible. The German merchant fleet was not large enough to carry millions of Jews to Madagascar. All of the Third Reich's merchant ships were needed to transport troops and military equipment. In addition, the British Royal Navy, the world's dominant sea power, would have prevented German ships from sailing with their human cargo.

Would lives have been saved if the Madagascar Plan had been put into operation? Perhaps fewer Jews would have died in the gas chambers. But if life in the European ghettos is any indication, conditions in a Madagascar ghetto would have been just as appalling.

they approached," writes survivor Leo Fettman. "Everyone in the boxcar fell silent as the heavy door rolled open. I was standing near the door and could see hundreds of confused, frightened people already standing on the platform alongside the train."[12] The SS guards were an intimidating sight to the Jews as they disembarked. Dressed in spotless uniforms, carrying whips and accompanied by snarling attack dogs, the SS men strutted up and down the platform shouting orders to the newly arrived deportees. Everything was done with much commotion and speed to crush the spirits of the new arrivals and make them more compliant to the guards' commands. Oskar Berger recalls a scene of stark horror when his train arrived at Treblinka:

> As we disembarked we witnessed a horrible sight: hundreds of bodies lying all around. Piles of bundles, clothes, valises, everything mixed together. SS soldiers, Germans, and Ukrainians were standing on the roofs of the barracks, and firing indiscriminately into the crowd. Men, women, and children fell bleeding. The air was filled with screaming and weeping. Those not wounded by the shooting were forced through an open gate, jumping over the dead and wounded, to a square fenced in by barbed wire.[13]

Soon the platforms were empty. The Jews had been marched to their predetermined fates in the gas chambers. The corpses of those who had died on the train or had been shot by the guards were scooped up and tossed in trucks and driven away, to be disposed of like common refuse. Although the station was now quiet, before long another train full of Jews would arrive, then another, and another: a seemingly endless procession of the doomed to be intimidated, processed, and murdered as Hitler's Final Solution rolled on.

> "Soldiers entered the car and robbed us and even cut off fingers with rings. They claimed that we didn't need them any more."[11]
>
> —Holocaust survivor Ada Lichtman.

CHAPTER TWO

Slaves of the Reich

The German words *Arbeit Macht Frei* over the entrance of several Holocaust camps seemed to hold promise for the new prisoners who marched through the gate. In English, the words mean "Work Makes You Free," and those who entered under this sign hoped that it was true. They believed that if they worked hard for the Nazis they would eventually be set free. But the sign was a blatant lie that dangled false hope before the eyes of the captives. Those who were able would be forced to work, but in most cases that work would bring death, not freedom.

At the 1942 Wannsee Conference Reinhard Heydrich discussed the use of Jewish and other prisoners as a source of labor for the Reich. Notes taken at the meeting describe Heydrich's plan for putting the Jews to work:

> Under proper guidance, in the course of the final solution the Jews are to be allocated for appropriate labor in the East. Able-bodied Jews, separated according to sex, will be taken in large work columns to these areas for work on roads, in the course of which action doubtless a large portion will be eliminated by natural causes. The possible final remnant will, since it will undoubtedly consist of the most resistant portion, have to be treated accordingly, because it is the product of natural selection and would, if released, act as the seed of a new Jewish revival.[14]

Although couched in seemingly innocuous words, Heydrich's meaning was clear to those sitting around the conference table: Most Jews would work themselves to death; the rest would be killed to prevent any chance of an uprising. As a nation at war, Germany needed as many workers as possible to provide not only the weapons and ammunition needed for the war effort but also consumer goods for the

German people. With so many of Germany's young and healthy sons sent off to fight, the Jewish prisoners represented a readily available source of labor.

Between 1940 and 1943 more than one hundred *Arbeitslagern*, or labor camps, were established in Germany and its occupied territories to take advantage of Jewish slave labor. Smaller subcamps were built around many of the major camps to provide laborers for nearby factories and other work sites. During the course of the war millions of prisoners worked and died for Hitler's Third Reich.

An Army of Slaves

Even before the Nazis created camps specifically for slave labor, they were already putting prisoners to work in concentration camps. Dachau, located near a town of the same name, was the first Nazi concentration camp. It opened on March 22, 1933, just weeks after Hitler came to power. Constructed at an abandoned munitions plant, Dachau originally housed political prisoners, homosexuals, and Jehovah's Witnesses (who, as pacifists, opposed Germany's aggression).

The camp's population that first year numbered less than five thousand. At first few Jews were interned at the camp, but as the persecution of Jews increased throughout the 1930s more were sent to Dachau. Approximately two hundred thousand prisoners were interned at Dachau between 1933 and 1945 in both the main camp and its more than one hundred subcamps. Dachau became the model for subsequent camps constructed by the Nazis.

> "Able-bodied Jews, separated according to sex, will be taken in large work columns to these areas for work on roads, in the course of which action doubtless a large portion will be eliminated by natural causes."[14]
> —SS general Reinhard Heydrich.

The main component of the daily routine for the majority of prisoners at Dachau was work. "Prisoners, without exception, are obligated to carry out physical labor,"[15] ordered Theodor Eicke, SS commander of the camp. Prisoners worked on the construction of several of the camp's buildings or assisted in the daily operation of the camp. The Labor Allocation Office, which assigned men to *Kommandos*, or work details, was run entirely by prisoners. Much of the work, however, was located outside the camp's barbed wire fences. Each day at dawn prisoners in a *Kommando* were escorted through the main gate, under the *Arbeit Macht Frei* sign, to their work assignments. The jobs allocated to the prisoners were varied. Some men went to work in factories in the town of Dachau, while others labored in a local meat-packing plant. Some were sent to labor at Kiesgrube, a gravel pit, or to a nearby experimental herb farm called the *Plantages*. The treatment of Jewish prisoners at Dachau was especially cruel. According to one who survived, "The Jewish prisoners worked in special detachments and received the hardest tasks. They were beaten at every opportunity."[16] The average life expectancy of a Jewish prisoner in the camps was only four months.

> "The Jewish prisoners worked in special detachments and received the hardest tasks. They were beaten at every opportunity."[16]
>
> —Dachau survivor.

Although conditions at Dachau were not as harsh as they would become at later camps, brutality and death were still the constant companions of the prisoners. An official US Army report on the liberation of Dachau in 1945 includes some chilling facts about the work details.

It is estimated that approximately 3,000 Jews died on the *Plantages*. When the camp officials felt that these internees were too ill and too weak to work, they would march them into a lake (since drained), regardless of the time of year. They were forced to stay in the water until dead. Those who remained conscious were placed in wheelbarrows, brought back to camp, where they died a few hours later.

The Kiesgrube detail was considered the worst work detail the internees could be put on. They would have to load wagons with crushed rock at a speed which caused the internees to collapse and die on the spot.[17]

Supervision of the camp workers was often delegated by a camp's SS overseers to other prisoners. Called *Kapos*, these prisoner-supervisors were often the most brutal of the inmates, carrying out their cruel tasks in exchange for certain privileges granted to them by the SS. Many Kapos were Jews and thus considered traitors by other Jewish prisoners. Kapos were exempt from hard labor and had better food and living quarters. Their abusive actions often stemmed from the fear of

Prisoners in striped uniforms are forced to work on a construction crew at Sachsenhausen concentration camp in the 1930s. As at Dachau and other camps, the slogan Arbeit Macht Frei (Work Makes You Free) *appeared at the entrance to Sachsenhausen.*

Identity in the Camps

Part of the practice of humiliating prisoners in the Holocaust camps was the stripping away of their identities. Every prisoner wore the same striped uniform, and names were irrelevant to the SS guards who called their charges "dogs" and "swine."

Although they were not seen as individuals, prisoners were usually identified according to the reason they were imprisoned. This was represented by colored triangles sewn point down on the inmates' uniforms, each color identifying a specific group:

Red: Political prisoners (Communists, labor unionists, socialists)

Green: Habitual criminals

Black: "Asocials" (mentally ill, alcoholics, vagrants, etc.)

Purple: Jehovah's Witnesses

Pink: Homosexuals, sex offenders

Brown: Gypsies (Roma and Sinti)

Blue: Foreign laborers, emigrants

Letters were sometimes printed on a triangle to denote a prisoner's nationality; for example, "F" for France, "P" for Poland, "I" for Italy. Jewish prisoners generally wore two yellow triangles forming a six-pointed Star of David, the traditional symbol of the Jewish faith.

being stripped of their special status and returned to the ranks of the ordinary workers. Laborers were sometimes treated like animals, as Primo Levi recalls: "Some of them [the Kapos] beat us from pure bestiality and violence, but others beat us when we are under a load almost lovingly, accompanying the blows with exhortations, as cart-drivers do with willing horses."[18]

Laboring at Ravensbrück

Women also toiled in the camps, sometimes alongside their male counterparts. Initially their jobs involved cleaning, cooking, and caring for sick or injured prisoners. Later they were forced to perform labor as demanding and exhausting as that of the men. About 50 miles (80.4 km) north of Berlin, a camp called Ravensbrück was established for women prisoners. Seren Tuvel, then age twenty-six, recalls standing in a large, bare room with some thirty other women. Their hair roughly shorn and their jewelry confiscated, they wore coarse, ill-fitting garments that were too thin to protect them from the cold. A uniformed female guard stepped to the front of the room and addressed the women. "You are now in Ravensbrück, an all-women camp. There are no men here except for a few doctors in the hospital. You are our first Jewish prisoners."[19] Ravensbrück was the only Holocaust camp specifically established for women, but it was no less brutal than other camps. Many of the female guards employed by the SS were criminals. "In case you're wondering why I'm here . . . I'm a criminal," announced the guard in front of Tuvel's group. "Does anyone want to know what I did? I killed someone . . . stabbed her with a knife. Anything else you want to know?"[20]

Ravensbrück was constructed in 1938, and an initial contingent of 867 women were interned there in 1939. By the time Tuvel arrived in 1944 it housed some eighty thousand women

> "The Kiesgrube detail was considered the worst work detail the internees could be put on. They would have to load wagons with crushed rock at a speed which caused the internees to collapse and die on the spot."[17]
>
> —Official US Army report.

as well as hundreds of children. The daily routine for most of the women of Ravensbrück was work. At roll call, which sometimes began as early as 4:00 a.m., prisoners lined up outdoors (often for hours) while the guards made sure no one had escaped overnight. After roll call the women were marched to work their usual twelve-hour day. Tuvel recalls her job unloading ships that docked some three miles from camp.

> On reaching the ship we climbed up a ramp leading to the deck and immediately were ordered to carry crates of

vegetables back down the ramp and up a small hill to the *Kartoffelkeller* [food storage cellar]. . . . We worked in pairs, each woman holding a handle at either end of a wooden crate as we walked down the ramp and up the hill. . . . Every day, seven days a week, we unloaded and sorted until late in the afternoon, and were then marched back to the camp.[21]

After another roll call the women were finally allowed to return to their barracks for the evening meal: watery soup and a morsel of bread baked with sawdust. Tuvel's job unloading vegetables had a small benefit: It allowed her to secretly eat a radish or carrot when the guards were not looking. Soon she began sneaking a few vegetables back to the barracks to supplement the camp food or to trade with Gentile prisoners, who received better rations than the Jews. After a night of fitful sleep in crowded bunks the routine began all over again the next morning. As the women lined up for roll call they saw bodies stacked like cordwood outside the barracks—victims of overwork and exposure.

Jobs at Ravensbrück and its subcamps varied greatly. Some women altered confiscated clothing for use by the German war effort. They sewed uniforms, coats, and gloves for the SS and the *Wehrmacht* (armed forces) in a textile factory built within the Ravensbrück compound. Others shoveled coal and constructed roads and buildings. Still others worked in German factories such as the electrical engineering firm Siemens and Halske, where women made electronic parts for Nazi weaponry. Working conditions for women were no better than conditions for men at other labor camps. Prisoners who were no longer productive were gassed, or shot, or subjected to medical experiments from which they never recovered. Between fifty thousand and ninety thousand prisoners died at Ravensbrück.

The Tunnels of Mittelbau-Dora

While the women of Ravensbrück sewed uniforms and made parts for weapons, other slave laborers were working on a secret weapon that Hitler believed would turn the tide of war. Although his *Luftwaffe* (air force) bombers had been unable to pound England into submission, Hitler's new weapon, a guided missile called the V-2, could de-

Female inmates of Auschwitz, their heads shorn, march to a work site. Women prisoners at Ravensbrück and other camps worked long days, ate substandard food, and suffered from exposure to cold weather.

liver explosives to enemy territory without putting pilots at risk. But Allied air power threatened the factory at Peenemünde, Germany, where the Nazis were scrambling to complete their new missile. Beginning in 1943 Germany was subjected to an intense campaign of air strikes by Allied bombers. Targeting the industrial might of the Third Reich, American bombers dropped their deadly loads during the day, followed by British bombing raids at night. Aircraft factories, oil refineries, and rail lines all suffered major damage from the constant aerial bombardment. Just before the V-2 manufacturing facility at Peenemünde was to begin operating, a British air raid killed two scientists and damaged the production plant. To avoid losses from future raids, manufacture of the V-2 was moved to a series of tunnels beneath a mountain near Nordhausen, Germany.

IG Farben: War Profiteer

The Third Reich required a vast system of industries to provide the weapons, uniforms, chemicals, and thousands of other vital commodities needed for World War II. The war was immensely profitable for manufacturers that supplied the Nazi military machine. The largest of these companies was German chemical giant IG Farben.

Founded in 1925, IG Farben had become the largest chemical company in the world by World War II. Among the products IG Farben or its subsidiaries produced were a synthetic rubber called "buna" (used for vehicle tires, hoses, and other industrial applications), explosives, and a pesticide called Zyklon B. In 1942 the company made a deal with the SS to build a factory at Auschwitz (later known as Auschwitz III or Monowitz). IG Farben made huge profits from tax incentives granted by the Nazis and from the labor of thousands of slaves from Auschwitz. It is doubtful that the Nazis could have sustained their war effort without IG Farben. Its tires and oil products were essential for military vehicles, while Zyklon B was used to kill thousands of innocent prisoners.

Such a vital industry was bound to become a prime target for Allied bombers. Beginning in August 1944 air raids pounded the facility for four months; Auschwitz was finally liberated by the Soviets in January 1945. After the war IG Farben was dismantled and many of its executives tried and convicted of war crimes. Although IG Farben is gone, some of its subsidiaries (including Bayer Aspirin) are still making products.

Originally built by a mining company, the tunnel system had to be expanded for V-2 production. Just ten days after the bombing of Peenemünde, the first slave laborers arrived from the Buchenwald concentration camp. Established as a subcamp of Buchenwald, the tunnel facility was given the name Dora. Later the name Mittelbau (meaning central construction) was added. As in other labor camps, the prisoners at Dora were subjected to backbreaking work and inhumane living conditions. About sixty thousand prisoners worked in the tunnels; one-third of those died from overwork, disease, starvation, or execution. Prisoners assembled the missiles on two winding, s-shaped assembly lines. The workers were divided into two groups: transport workers who carried missile components through the tunnels, and specialists who assembled and tested the finished rocket. Kapos in the tunnels made sure the prisoners kept on schedule, mercilessly beating those who faltered.

The first V-2 was launched against Paris in September 1944. Strikes against targets in Great Britain, Belgium, France, and the Netherlands followed over the next five months. More than 6,000 V-2 missiles were manufactured, with 3,225 launched against Allied cities. It is an irony of history that more slave laborers died building the V-2 rockets than civilians died in thousands of V-2 missile attacks.

Extermination by Labor

While the Nazis needed slave laborers from the camps to support their war effort, they also had to keep in mind that a primary goal of the war was the annihilation of what they termed *the Jewish race*. The slaves had to be kept alive long enough to do the necessary work, yet killing them was also a priority. These two outcomes were unified in the Nazi concept of "extermination by labor." Heavy labor such as road-building, quarrying, and construction was, by its very nature, demanding. When minimal food rations, brutal physical punishment, long working hours in all types of weather, and little rest were added, the result was predictable: Workers died. In 1938 a labor camp was constructed in Austria to exemplify the principle of extermination by labor.

The camp was located near the Austrian town of Mauthausen. The main purpose of the camp was to work its prisoners to death; useful production was merely a secondary result. Conditions at Mauthausen were so severe that inmates at other concentration camps dreaded being sent there. Prisoners were sent to work twelve hours a day in Wiener Graben, a nearby stone quarry operated by the SS. They were forced to work in the quarry with only their bare hands or primitive tools. When inmates could no longer work they were killed at the camp's gas chamber and cremated in ovens that ran twenty-four hours a day.

One particularly dreaded feature of the quarry was a long, steep stairway cut into the granite wall. According to Felix Landau, whose father worked there,

> The rock quarry was at the base of the infamous "Stairs of Death." Prisoners had to carry one-hundred-pound stone blocks . . . up the 186 stairs to the top of the cliff. They climbed in continuous rows, four across. If anyone dropped or collapsed, he caused all behind him to fall in a domino effect. For sadistic amusement, the Nazis often forced prisoners to race up the stairs carrying blocks of stone.[22]

Inmates at Mauthausen who were too weak or too sick to work were killed in the gas chambers and then cremated in ovens that ran around the clock. Pictured is one of the ovens in Mauthausen's crematorium.

As at other camps, Jews received the worst treatment at Mauthausen. Indiscriminate beatings were common. The SS guards took great delight in pushing Jews some 200 feet (60.9 m) to their deaths off the top ledge of the quarry in an area that they mockingly named the "Parachute Jump." In 1941 a group of Dutch Jews were forced to run up and down the steps with stone blocks on their backs. For two days the number of Jews dwindled as the cruel game claimed the prisoners' lives. On the third day those who survived carrying rocks up and down the steps committed suicide by jumping off the cliff. According to the US Holocaust Memorial Museum, some ninety-five thousand prisoners died at Mauthausen, more than fourteen thousand of them Jews.

Without the slave labor of the Holocaust camps, Nazi Germany could not have sustained its war effort for as long as it did. Hundreds of German firms benefitted from such labor, including auto makers BMW, Audi, and Volkswagen; electronics firm AEG/Telefunken; and military equipment manufacturer Krupp. Although no amount of money could adequately compensate for the horrors of the labor camps, in 1999, sixteen German corporations established a $1.7 billion fund for the surviving slave laborers.

CHAPTER THREE

Human Guinea Pigs

One of the most important components of the Nazi war machine was the *Luftwaffe*. When a *Luftwaffe* plane was shot down in combat, the pilot sometimes had to parachute into the freezing waters of the North Sea. This often resulted in death by hypothermia, or extreme cold. After the invasion of the Soviet Union in 1941 the German army became bogged down in the blizzards and below-zero temperatures of the brutal Russian winter. "The cold was, quite simply, a killer," writes German soldier Siegfried Knapp. "We were all in danger of freezing to death."[23]

Nazi doctors had to find ways to improve the survival rate of Germany's aviators and soldiers. So they turned to the Holocaust camps for a virtually unlimited supply of human guinea pigs for their experiments.

Lethal Medicine

Medical research played a three-fold purpose in the Third Reich. Along with seeking ways to improve the survival rate of German soldiers, Nazi physicians also tested experimental drugs and surgical procedures on prisoners and conducted research designed to confirm the validity of Nazi racial ideology. Between 1941 and the end of the war in 1945 at least seventy research projects involving thousands of gruesome medical procedures were carried out on prisoners in numerous camps. The victims were mostly Jews, although Roma, Poles, and other non-Jewish inmates were also subjected to Nazi medical experiments. Doctors conducted procedures without the consent (and in some cases, without the knowledge) of the prisoners and with no regard for the suffering and ultimate death of their subjects.

These experiments took place in Dachau, Mauthausen, Buchenwald, Auschwitz-Birkenau, and other camps. They included infecting prisoners with diseases such as tuberculosis and malaria, performing unnecessary surgery and amputations without anesthetics, exposing victims to toxic gas, and dissecting living inmates. Prisoners who somehow managed to live through the experiments were usually killed once they were no longer needed. The numbers vary, but between seven thousand and eighteen thousand prisoners died in agony as a result of the medical experiments. Nearly two hundred Nazi doctors were involved in unethical medical experimentation, although only a small fraction of them were brought to trial after the war. For the Nazi physicians, the guiding principle of medical ethics—to do no harm to their patients—was replaced by the Nazi concept of Aryan superiority over all other people.

Conquering Height and Cold

One of the physicians who conducted human experiments for the Nazis was Sigmund Rascher, a captain in the SS and a friend of SS chief Heinrich Himmler. With the advent of World War II, Rascher joined the *Luftwaffe* and became interested in the consequences of extreme altitude on living organisms. His goal was to determine the highest altitude a *Luftwaffe* pilot could parachute from without suffering damaging effects. Previous German experiments of this type used monkeys as test subjects. Recognizing that human subjects would be more suitable than animals for such studies, Rascher wrote to Himmler, "Can you make available two or three professional criminals for these experiments? . . . The experiments, from which the subjects can, of course, die, would take place with my cooperation."[24] Of course the "professional criminals" referred to were concentration camp inmates.

In the spring of 1942 Rascher had a special low-pressure chamber installed at Dachau, and soon thereafter the experiments began. Test subjects were placed in the chamber and the air removed to simulate the thinner atmosphere at high altitudes. The following is part of Rascher's account of one such experiment, taken from transcripts of the postwar Nuremburg Trials.

> It was a continuous experiment without oxygen at a height of 12 km conducted on a 37 year old Jew in good general condition. Breathing continued up to 30 minutes. After 4 minutes

the VP [test person] began to perspire and to wiggle his head, after 5 minutes cramps occurred, between 6 and 10 minutes breathing increased in speed and the VP became unconscious, after 11 to 30 minutes breathing slowed down to three breaths per minute, finally stopping altogether.[25]

An autopsy was then performed to determine the effects of high altitude on the man's internal organs. Most test subjects suffered horribly with convulsions, ruptured lungs, and burst eardrums. Ac-

A series of photographs, taken by German doctors in the 1930s, shows the effects of compression and decompression in experiments carried out on a prisoner. Most prisoners subjected to pressure chamber experiments died; the others were killed when the experiments ended.

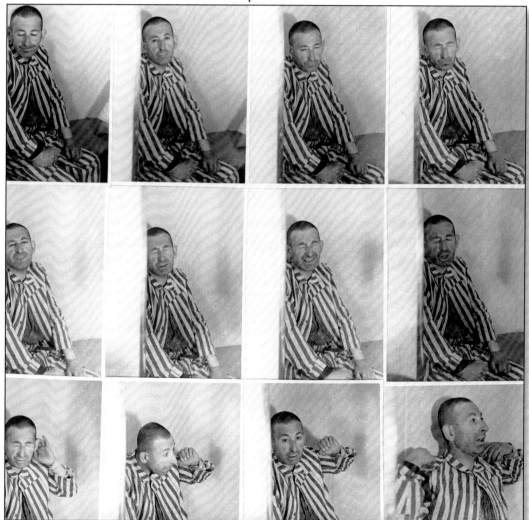

Operation T4

Nazi physicians made detailed measurements of prisoners to identify men and women with desirable genetic traits for breeding a new master race. Along with increasing the Aryan population, the Nazis also wanted to decrease the number of people who did not measure up to the Aryan ideal. In 1939 Adolf Hitler ordered the establishment of a project to accomplish this goal. It went by the name Operation T4.

The objective of Operation T4 was to rid the Third Reich of all people it characterized as *lebensunwerten lebens* (life unworthy of life). These included people with physical disabilities, mental illnesses, a variety of chronic illnesses, and people classified as criminally insane. German hospitals, nursing homes, and psychiatric institutions were required to complete a form for each patient. The Operation T4 doctors then evaluated the forms, marking each with either a red plus sign for death, or a blue minus sign for life. Those marked for death were transported to one of several euthanasia centers, where they were killed. Doctors used lethal injections at first, later murdering their victims in gas chambers and disposing of the bodies in crematoria.

Deception was key in Operation T4. Death certificates of the victims were falsified. Relatives of the murdered patients were told their loved ones had died of a disease and had been cremated quickly to prevent danger to the public. More than seventy thousand people were murdered during Operation T4, a chilling preview of the Holocaust killing centers to come.

cording to one witness, they "would go mad and pull out their hair in an effort to relieve the pressure. They would beat the walls with their hands and head, and scream."[26] Some two hundred prisoners underwent such high-altitude experiments; eighty died from the tests, and the remaining were murdered.

Rascher's tests on human subjects exposed to extreme cold were just as cruel as his experiments with altitude. Starting in August 1942

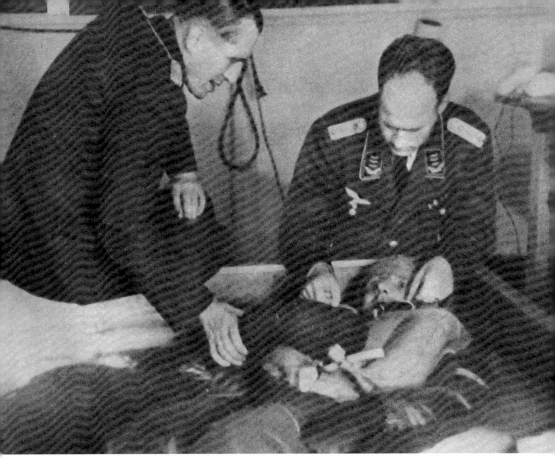

Nazi physicians check the vital signs of a Dachau concentration camp prisoner who is immersed in freezing water. He wears a life jacket to prevent drowning.

Rasher ordered prisoners to be immersed for hours in a tank of water while wearing a *Luftwaffe* flying suit. They also wore a life jacket—to prevent drowning. According to one of Rascher's reports on these tests, the water in the tanks varied from 36.5° to 53.6° F (2.5° to 12° C). When the prisoners lost consciousness as their internal temperatures plummeted, Rascher and his assistants performed blood tests and monitored the victims' temperature, heart rate, and other vital signs. Normal human body temperature is 98.6° F (37° C); the body temperatures of the test subjects fell to approximately 80° F (26.7° C). Rascher noted that subjects whose neck and back of the head were submerged always died. Attempts were made to revive the victims using hot baths, sun lamps, and heated sleeping bags, but all resuscitation efforts failed. As many as one hundred prisoners died as a result of these grotesque experiments.

The effects of dry cold suffered by German troops on the Russian front presented Rascher with yet another challenge. For these tests, inmates were left naked outdoors on metal carts in freezing cold for periods of up to fourteen hours. The screams of pain from these test subjects as they froze were so horrific that it was once suggested the experiments be moved from Dachau to the larger Auschwitz camp, where the tests could be performed in more isolated areas. When the victims became unconscious, their vital signs were recorded, and then they were tossed into tanks of warm (sometimes boiling) water to see if they could be revived. Some lived, but most perished.

Fighting Disease

Ethical doctors strive to heal their patients by administering medicine to cure disease and relieve suffering. The doctors in the Nazi camps operated in exactly the opposite manner, using prisoners as test subjects for evaluating the effects of deadly diseases on the human body. Such experiments were carried out with no regard for the welfare of the subjects, and the outcome was usually death or permanent disability.

Malaria, an infectious disease transmitted to humans by mosquitoes, can cause flu-like symptoms, yellowing of the skin, and coma or death. It was one of the diseases most commonly found in Nazi-occupied territories. From 1942 to 1945 experiments to develop a malaria vaccine were conducted at Dachau by Claus Schilling, a specialist in tropical diseases. More than one thousand relatively healthy prisoners were infected with the disease, either by mosquitoes or by blood transfusions from inmates who already had malaria. Inmate Leo Miechalowski was infected by mosquitoes contained in cages. "I had to put my hand on one of the little cages and a mosquito stung me, and afterwards I was still in the hospital for five weeks."[27] Miechalowski eventually contracted malaria and was given numerous injections of anti-malarial drugs. The treatment was worse than the disease. "All of a sudden," recalls Miechalowski, "my heart felt like it was going to be torn out. I became insane. I completely lost my language—my ability to speak."[28] Miechalowski recovered, but many others were not so fortunate. Some three hundred to four hundred prisoners died in the experiments, most succumbing to the treatments rather than the disease.

Finding a cure for typhus, another deadly disease, was the focus of experiments performed at Buchenwald. Patients with typhus experience severe muscle pain, high fever, and delirium; without treatment, the disease can be fatal. Some one thousand inmates were infected with typhus at the camp's isolated research station called Block 46. Prisoner Eugen Kogon recalls that those who were sent to Block 46 could "expect death and under certain circumstances, a very long drawn out and frightful death."[29] After infection, some of the patients were given vaccines made from lice, dog and rabbit lungs, and mouse livers. Treatment was withheld from other prisoners, called passage persons, who were used as a source of the disease to infect others. As with most Nazi medical experiments, the typhus tests resulted in no useful medical breakthroughs. As many as four hundred test subjects died from the experiments in Block 46.

> "All of a sudden my heart felt like it was going to be torn out. I became insane. I completely lost my language—my ability to speak."[28]
>
> —Medical test subject Leo Miechalowski.

Surgical Atrocities

Battlefield wounds caused enormous losses for the *Wehrmacht*, and the Nazi doctors designed experiments to test methods of accelerating the healing of injuries. Some of the most sadistic and excruciating of these experiments were performed on the women of Ravensbrück. To find out how bones, nerves, and muscles regenerated after an injury, doctors at Ravensbrück devised numerous painful procedures. They used hammers to break the leg bones of female victims, then fastened the broken pieces together and applied plaster casts. Similarly, portions of thigh and calf muscles were repeatedly cut out, each time removing larger pieces. The wounds were then dressed, but infection usually set in because the dressings were seldom changed. Although anesthesia was sometimes administered, most of the operations were performed without painkillers. After undergoing these procedures, the subjects suffered severe pain, high fevers, and crippling deformities. In another Ravensbrück experiment, doctors amputated the arms and legs of women who were deemed mentally ill. The limbs were then packed in sterile dressings and sent to Hohenlychen, a nearby hospital for convalescing German soldiers, to see if successful transplants could be made. The donors of the amputated limbs were killed and their bodies dumped in mass graves or cremated.

To test the effectiveness of the antibacterial drug sulfanilamide, Nazi doctors simulated infected battlefield wounds by making inci-

The Ethics of Nazi Experimentation

The fact that Nazi medical experiments were atrocities performed on innocent people is beyond debate. Most of these experiments were medically worthless and used merely as excuses to torture and kill Jews. Some, however, managed to produce useful medical findings. Should such information be used in today's medical research? Or do the methods used to obtain these results taint them forever?

In 1984 Canadian biology professor John Hayward studied hypothermia using data from Nazi experiments. "I don't want to have to use the Nazi data," Hayward remarked, "but there is no other and will be no other in an ethical world. I've rationalized it a bit. But not to use it would be equally bad. I'm trying to make something constructive out of it." Hayward is not alone—numerous scientific publications have referenced Nazi experiments in the postwar years. But the controversy remains. The head of the US Environmental Protection Agency refused to let his organization use Nazi data in its research on poisonous phosgene gas, citing ethical concerns and doubts about the scientific value of the Nazi experiments.

Can good come from evil? Some say that using Nazi medical data is the final indignity for the thousands who died horrible deaths as human guinea pigs. Many argue that such use could encourage new atrocities. Others respond that ignoring information that could help people simply because of its origin serves no useful purpose. This debate will undoubtedly persist.

Quoted in Baruch C. Cohen, "The Ethics of Using Medical Data from Nazi Experiments," Jewish Law. www.jlaw.com.

sions in the legs of prisoners, inserting bacteria-laden glass or wood slivers into the wound, and then sewing up the incision. When the inevitable infection set in, doctors applied sulfanilamide to some patients, withholding it from others to form a control group. On some prisoners doctors stopped circulation in the limb by tying off blood vessels to more accurately simulate bullet wounds. As one test subject recalls, "I felt severe pain and blood flowed from my leg. At night we were all alone without any care. I heard only the screaming of my fellow prisoners, and I heard also that they asked for water. There was nobody to give us any water or bed pans."[30]

> "[Inmates of Block 46 could] expect death and under certain circumstances, a very long drawn out and frightful death."[29]
>
> —Prisoner Eugen Kogon.

The Nazis had no qualms about conducting such horrendous tests on human beings; they justified their actions by saying they were searching for ways to save German lives on the battlefield. But some experiments were designed expressly for the purpose of watching people die. Prisoners at Buchenwald were fed poisoned food or shot with poison-tipped bullets to determine how long it took various toxins to kill. Other inmates were given a drug designed to stop bleeding, and then were shot to determine the effectiveness of the drug. All the test subjects died within a short period of time, and autopsies were then performed. It was simply murder under the guise of medical research.

Creating a Master Race

One of Hitler's dreams for the Third Reich was to build a society where the superior Aryan race would control the world, while inferior races would be enslaved or eliminated. Even before World War II doctors in the Third Reich attempted to determine what physical traits characterized the typical Aryan. They collected measurements on people of various backgrounds to gather such data as nose length and width, angle of the ears, and hair and eye color, and categorized them as either Aryan or non-Aryan. As the number of Holocaust camps grew in the 1940s, doctors gained an ample supply of patients on whom to perform even more radical experiments. One of the most notorious of all the doctors performing these experiments was a handsome young Nazi physician named Josef Mengele.

Mengele had always been interested in genetics. He had degrees in anthropology and medicine. As an officer in the SS he had also served on the Russian front, where he earned a medal for being wounded in combat. In 1943 Mengele arrived at Auschwitz to further his study of genetics. Along with some thirty other camp doctors, Mengele was charged with separating newly arrived prisoners who were fit for work from those who would be put to death immediately. The inmates hated his coldly callous attitude, as revealed by the comments of a female prisoner: "How we despised his detached, haughty air, his continual whistling, his absurd orders, his frigid cruelty!"[31] For his attitude displayed during the selection process, Mengele earned the nickname "Angel of Death."

One area that especially interested Mengele was research in the genetics of twins. By studying twin children he sought to learn which traits were inherited and which developed as a result of one's upbringing. His goal was to determine how to enhance traits such as

Identical twins Jiri and Josef Fiser of Czechoslovakia were subjected to the experiments of Josef Mengele, the Nazi doctor who had a fascination with genetics and twins. Mengele conducted many bizarre and cruel experiments on twins.

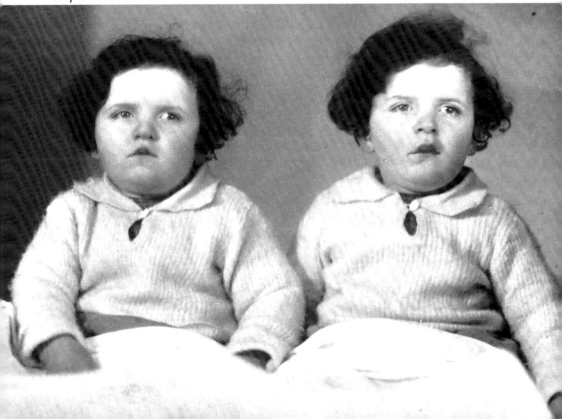

blue eyes, trim physical build, and narrow nose—all of which fit the Nazi ideal of superior Aryan children. As families arrived at Auschwitz he prowled the train platform, personally selecting young twins for his experiments, shouting *"Zwillinge heraus!"*[32] (Twins out!) Because Mengele needed healthy test subjects he made sure that his twins enjoyed better food and more livable quarters. In many instances he kept twins from being sent to death in the gas chambers. Once he had selected his subjects, Mengele spent hours examining, measuring, drawing blood samples, and inquiring about their family history. Such examinations often went on for months while Mengele and his assistants gathered data.

> "Since it was necessary to perform a dissection for the simultaneous evaluation of anomalies, the twins had to die at the same time. So it was that they met their death . . . at the hands of Dr. Mengele."[33]
>
> —Jewish physician and Auschwitz prisoner Miklos Nyiszli.

Cruel Experiments

After the relatively harmless testing and measuring were finished, more sinister experiments began. Mengele's experimentation on children rivaled the cruelty of tests performed by other Nazi doctors on adult prisoners. Some tests depended on comparing the physiological differences between twins. Miklos Nyiszli, a Jewish doctor and Auschwitz prisoner who assisted Mengele, later described the nature of these tests in a memoir of his time in the camp.

Here it was a question of comparing the twins' healthy organs with those functioning abnormally, or of comparing their illnesses. For that study, as it was for all studies of pathological nature, corpses were needed. Since it was necessary to perform a dissection for the simultaneous evaluation of anomalies, the twins had to die at the same time. So it was that they met their death . . . at the hands of Dr. Mengele.[33]

For some of these experiments, one twin was infected with a disease such as typhus while the other twin remained healthy. After the first twin became ill, both were killed and autopsies undertaken.

Amputations and other unnecessary surgical procedures were also performed, as were blood transfusions from one twin to his or her sibling, or to other prisoners. Children were killed by injections of chloroform directly into their hearts so that they could be autopsied or experimented on and their organs sent to Berlin for further study. At least one report tells of twins sewed together back to back in an effort to create Siamese twins (the commonly used term for conjoined twins) for study. Of the thousands of children who underwent these horrible tests, only a few hundred survived.

Nazi medical experimentation was one of the most horrific aspects of the Holocaust. As scientific research it was a sham, and the majority of its results were worthless. The main accomplishment of the experiments was the torture and death of thousands of innocent victims.

CHAPTER FOUR

The Killing Grounds

As the man who laid out the plans for Hitler's Final Solution and created the *Einsatzgruppen* (elite squads formed for the purpose of killing civilians in conquered territories), Reinhard Heydrich had proved himself one of the most feared men in the Third Reich. Even Hitler called him "the man with the iron heart."[34] But as merciless as he was, Heydrich was not immortal. In May 1942, he was assassinated by two Czech resistance fighters in the German-occupied city of Prague. Heinrich Himmler said, "It is our sacred obligation to avenge his death . . . and to destroy without mercy and weakness . . . the enemies of our people."[35] Revenge was swift, as German soldiers burned the Czech town of Lidice to the ground, bulldozing the rubble to eradicate all traces of the village. As for Heydrich, the Nazis accorded him one final honor: The program for building the killing centers that would destroy millions of Jewish lives was named after him.

Killing at Chelmno

Before the Wannsee Conference, Heydrich had authorized the creation of a killing center for Jews in Poland. The site for this first Nazi killing center was an abandoned estate (called the manor-house camp) in the Polish town of Chelmno and a clearing in the surrounding forest (the forest camp). The manor house contained rooms where prisoners undressed and deposited their valuables and a long central corridor that led the Jews and other prisoners to their deaths. Chelmno did not have a permanent gas chamber. Instead, the SS supervisors at the camp used specially modified "gas vans" to kill victims with carbon monoxide. Formerly ordinary trucks, the gas vans held from fifty to seventy prisoners in an airtight rear compartment. During a postwar trial, Chelmno SS guard Theodor Malzmüller described the killing process:

The back door of the van would be open. The Jews were made to get inside the van. . . . When all the Jews were inside the door was bolted. The driver then switched on the engine, crawled under the van and connected a pipe from the exhaust to the inside of the van. The exhaust fumes now poured into the inside of the truck so that the people inside were suffocated. After about ten minutes, when there were no further signs of life from the Jews, the van set off toward the camp in the woods where the bodies were then burnt.[36]

Extermination of Jews at Chelmno began in December 1941, and after a period of inactivity ceased operation as Soviet troops approached in January 1945. An estimated 150,000 to 180,000 people were murdered at Chelmno, including Jews, Poles, and Soviet prisoners of war. But for the number of Jews that Hitler planned to exterminate, Chelmno was not efficient enough. The Final Solution called for a permanent and well-organized system of extermination camps.

Operation Reinhard

In November 1941 construction began on a new killing center located near the Polish village of Belzec. It was the first of three camps built under the code name Operation Reinhard, the Nazi plan to exterminate the more than 2 million Jews in the General Government region of occupied Poland. To oversee the construction and operation of these camps, Heinrich Himmler assigned SS and Police Leader Odilo Globocnik to the task. Globocnik immediately began to lay out specifications for the new camps. The camps were constructed near rail lines to facilitate the transport of Jews and were located in isolated areas for secrecy, which was a major concern. "This is one of the most highly secret matters there are," Globocnik warned an SS engineer, "perhaps the most secret. Anybody who speaks about it is shot dead immediately."[37]

With gassing operations previously limited to the gas vans, Belzec became a testing ground for developing more efficient killing methods. Surrounded by barbed wire fences and trees that provided a measure of secrecy, Belzec was roughly square, approximately 900 feet (274.3 m) on each side. It was divided into two sections, with administration buildings and a railway spur and ramp on the western side and the killing facility on the eastern side. Within the administrative side were barracks for storing valuables and other goods seized from the prisoners, shoemaker and tailor shops for the camp's SS personnel, and barracks for prisoners to undress in before being gassed. The eastern section contained gas chambers, cremation pyres, and burial pits. Living quarters for the SS guards were located outside the camp's barbed wire fence. Killing operations at Belzec began on March 17, 1942, around the time the two other Reinhard camps were being constructed.

A monument in Lidice, Czech Republic, honors children killed in 1942 when German soldiers destroyed the town and killed its residents to avenge the assassination of Reinhard Heydrich by Czech resistance fighters. Before his death, Heydrich had authorized the first of the Nazi killing centers.

Sobibor and Treblinka

Using the knowledge gained from constructing Belzec the SS built two similarly designed extermination camps in the General Government region. The Sobibor camp in central Poland began gassing Jews in April 1942. Treblinka, the third Operation Reinhard camp, some 50 miles (80.5 km) northeast of Warsaw, opened in July 1942. Each camp was laid out and operated in a similar manner. The execution area was isolated from the other parts of the camps where SS men and prisoners worked and lived. High walls or earthen barriers kept prying eyes from viewing the killing operations. Each camp had a railroad platform where packed trains stopped to discharge their doomed passengers and where personal items (such as shoes, watches, and coats) confiscated from the Jews could be stored when they were sent into the gas chambers, which were also onsite.

"The appearance of the camp was like an ordinary farm, except for the barbed-wire fences that surrounded it and some barracks. Actually, it was a farm, with all its buildings, in the midst of a beautiful green forest."[38]

—A survivor of Sobibor.

The Nazis tried to make the camps look as innocuous as possible. None of the death apparatus could be seen from the train platform. A survivor of Sobibor recalls his first impression upon arrival: "The appearance of the camp was like an ordinary farm, except for the barbed-wire fences that surrounded it and some barracks. Actually, it was a farm, with all its buildings, in the midst of a beautiful green forest."[38] The railroad ramps, or platforms, inside the camps were made to resemble those of regular train stations. At Treblinka a sign greeted Jews leaving the trains:

Jews of Warsaw, Attention!

You are in a transit camp, from which you will be sent to a labor camp. In order to avoid epidemics, you must present your clothing and belongings for immediate disinfection. Gold, money, foreign currency, and jewelry should be deposited with the cashiers in return for a receipt. They will be returned to you later when you present the receipt. Bodily cleanliness requires that everyone bathe before continuing the journey.[39]

It was, of course, all a lie. The Jews would not be getting their possessions back, and the journey they were on led not to a labor camp but to the gas chambers.

Chambers of Death

Each of the three Operation Reinhard camps had gas chambers built specifically for the killing of human beings. At Belzec three chambers were constructed in a nondescript wooden barrack in the execution area of the camp. Each chamber had a large door with rubber gaskets to seal in the gas, secured by strong wooden bars on the outside to prevent escapes. The interiors of the chambers were made to resemble a shower room. SS sergeant Erich Fuchs, who assisted in the construction, later recalled, "I installed shower heads in the gas chambers. The nozzles were not connected to any water pipes; they would serve as camouflage for the gas chamber. For the Jews who were gassed it would seem as if they were being taken to baths and for disinfection."[40]

Each chamber had a pipe that led outside to the rear of the barrack, where it was attached to an engine taken from a captured Soviet tank. As at Chelmno, carbon monoxide exhaust was used to kill the Jews but on a larger scale not possible with the vans. In the first three months of Belzec's existence, some ninety-three thousand Jews died in its gas chambers. By June 1942 it became clear that the three gas chambers were not enough to handle the ever increasing trainloads of victims arriving at Belzec. The wooden barrack was demolished, and a new concrete structure containing six larger chambers was erected in its place. The chambers in this new building could handle the gassing of more than two thousand people at a time.

Carbon monoxide was also the killing method used at the other two Operation Reinhard camps. Sobibor, which began its killing program in May 1942 had three gas chambers built in a stone building, each connected to a tank engine in a shed outside. Each chamber held about two hundred people. Treblinka began operation with three gas chambers in July 1942. Ten more chambers were soon built when the capacity of the original three proved insufficient. Four thousand people could be gassed at one time in the new chambers.

Touching the Holocaust

When the Nazis evacuated the Sobibor killing center in 1943, they tried to destroy all evidence of its existence by demolishing the buildings and leveling the site. But in 2007 archaeologists began uncovering the camp's secrets that had been hidden for more than sixty years.

Israeli archaeologist Yoram Haimi began excavation at Sobibor after learning that two of his uncles died there. Haimi and Polish archaeologist Wojtek Mazurek mapped the camp's layout using ground-penetrating radar and satellite imaging. Careful digging uncovered numerous artifacts from the camp, including jewelry, medicine bottles, and household utensils. "We are touching the Holocaust," Haimi remarked.

In 2014 the archaeological team made a major breakthrough with the discovery of the foundations of Sobibor's gas chambers. By measuring the remains of these chambers, researchers will be able to more accurately determine the actual number of victims killed at Sobibor and gain valuable insight into the process that sent thousands to their deaths. Haimi was amazed by the size and state of preservation of the gas chambers. He was also moved by an artifact found near the chambers: a gold wedding band bearing a Hebrew inscription.

"Because of the lack of information about Sobibor," Haimi says, "every little piece of information is significant. No one knew where the gas chambers were. The Germans didn't want anyone to find out what was there. But thanks to what we have done, they didn't succeed."

Quoted in Matt Lebovic, "70 Years After Revolt, Sobibor Secrets Are Yet to Be Unearthed." *Times of Israel*, October 13, 2014. www.timesofisrael.com.

The Last March

All three Reinhard camps were soon operating at maximum capacity with minimum resistance from the victims. Upon arrival at the camp's station, the men were separated from the women and children. Some of the younger and healthier men from the trains were chosen to assist the

SS guards, while the others went into a barrack to be relieved of their clothing and valuables. The women and children were herded into a separate building for the same purpose. After undressing, the women's hair was cut and placed in bags to be used to make items for the German war effort, such as slippers for submarine crews. From that point on, everything was done quickly to prevent the victims from observing their surroundings and realizing what was about to happen to them.

A pile of shoes at Auschwitz concentration camp is but one reminder of the millions who died in Nazi death camps. Camp guards confiscated coats, shoes, watches, and other personal items from prisoners when they arrived and then sent them to their deaths in the gas chambers.

Connecting the undressing barracks with the gas chambers was a camouflaged path known as the "tube." It ranged in length from about 100 feet (30.5 m) at Belzec to almost 500 feet (152.4 m) at Sobibor. The tube was made from barbed wire fences, with branches intertwined to provide secrecy. The victims, men first, then women, were taken from the barracks and hurried along the tube toward the chambers. The victims' final march was a frightful one, as described years later by Jewish survivor Abraham Goldfarb:

> On the way to the gas chambers, on both sides of the fence, stood Germans with dogs. . . . The Germans beat the people with whips and iron bars so they would run and push to get into the "showers" quickly. The women's screams could be heard far off in other sections of the camp. The Germans urged the running victims on with yells of "Faster, faster, the water's getting cold, and others have to use the showers, too."[41]

When the chambers were full the doors were sealed and the tank engine started. After about twenty-five minutes all the victims were dead. Then Jewish workers opened the chamber doors and began removing the corpses and transporting them to nearby burial pits. Each camp had numerous burial pits for disposing of the remains of the Jews.

The Operation Reinhard camps, while efficient, could barely handle the sheer number of Jews to be exterminated. Two other camps in the General Government region, Auschwitz and Majdanek, also became part of the killing operations.

> "I installed shower heads in the gas chambers. The nozzles were not connected to any water pipes; they would serve as camouflage for the gas chamber. For the Jews who were gassed it would seem as if they were being taken to baths and for disinfection."[40]
>
> —SS sergeant Erich Fuchs.

Auschwitz

The name Auschwitz has become synonymous with the horrors of the Holocaust. The largest of the Holocaust camps, by 1944 it covered some 15.4 square miles (40 sq km). Auschwitz was composed of three parts: the main concentration camp, Auschwitz I; the killing center,

Auschwitz II (also called Auschwitz-Birkenau); and Auschwitz III (Monowitz or Buna), the forced labor camp. Construction on the main camp began in May 1940 on a former Polish military base. The other two camps were in operation by October 1942. Although Auschwitz I had a small gas chamber and crematorium, most of the killing was done at Auschwitz-Birkenau.

Upon arrival at Auschwitz, deportees immediately went through the selection process on the train platform, separating those fit to work from the others. As survivor Primo Levi recalls:

> In less than ten minutes, all the fit men had been collected together in a group. What happened to the others, to the women, to the children and to the old men, we could establish neither then nor later. . . . Today, however, we know that . . . of our convoy no more than ninety-six men and twenty-nine women entered the respective camps of Monowitz-Buna and Birkenau, and that of all the others, more than five hundred in number, not one was living two days later.[42]

Those five hundred victims went straight to the gas chambers to be killed by a new form of poison. Called Zyklon B (*Zyklon* is German for cyclone), it was a pesticide used to fumigate ships, railroad cars, buildings, and other enclosed spaces. Upon discovering that Zyklon B was lethal to animals, Nazi officials at Auschwitz tested it on a group of six hundred Soviet prisoners of war, with equally deadly results. Zyklon B became the toxin used at Auschwitz. Unlike the Operation Reinhard camps, there was no "tube" for victims to run through at Auschwitz-Birkenau. Jews and other prisoners selected for extermination were sent directly to the four crematorium buildings (known as Crematorium II, III, IV, and V) where the gas chambers were located. Deportees who were old, weak, or ill, were led into the crematorium by *Sonderkommandos*, work details of Jewish prisoners. "We

> "The Germans beat the people with whips and iron bars so they would run and push to get into the 'showers' quickly."[41]
>
> —Jewish prisoner Abraham Goldfarb.

Bombing Auschwitz

As Allied bombers flew devastating raids on German cities in 1944, a heated debate arose: Should the Allies bomb the Auschwitz killing center and the railroad lines that had brought so many Jews to their deaths?

There were strong arguments on both sides of the question. Some people wondered how Allied generals could do nothing while thousands of Jews were being sent to the gas chambers at Auschwitz every day. Others argued that not enough information about the camp was available to give a bombing raid a chance to succeed. Another side to the debate questioned whether killing innocent Jews in the camp was morally acceptable, even if it saved a greater number of lives. On August 20, 1944, Allied B-17 bombers dropped more than 1,000 bombs on the IG Farben synthetic oil factory; Auschwitz-Birkenau, less than 5 miles (8 km) away, was untouched.

In reality, the Allies did have information about Auschwitz-Birkenau. In April 1944 two Slovak Jews escaped from Auschwitz with detailed information about the camp and its operation. By June, Allied commanders had this valuable intelligence in hand. Despite repeated pleas from Jewish leaders, all plans for bombing Auschwitz were rejected. The official US position was that "the most effective relief to victims of enemy persecution is the early defeat of the Axis, an undertaking to which we must devote every resource at our disposal."

Quoted in David S. Wyman, "Why Auschwitz Wasn't Bombed," in Yisrael Gutman and Michael Berenbaum, eds., *Anatomy of the Auschwitz Death Camp*. Bloomington, IN: Indiana University Press, 1994, p. 572.

had to . . . take them inside the building," former *Sonderkommando* Shlomo Venezia writes, "to a place where an SS man was waiting to execute them in cold blood, one by one. For us, this was, by far, the most difficult task to accomplish."[43]

In the undressing rooms victims disrobed and turned over their valuables to the SS guards. Then they were led to the chambers and the doors sealed behind them. Eyewitnesses describe the killing process:

> Through an opening in the ceiling Germans dropped canisters into one of the wire mesh columns in the middle of the room. The canisters contained pellets of Zyklon B. . . . Each canister had four holes through which the gas escaped. The wire mesh columns prevented the prisoners from getting close enough to a canister to touch it with their hands; so the gas poured forth freely and asphyxiated them.[44]

Sonderkommandos use prongs to lift the corpse of a Dachau prisoner into a cremation oven. Prison details made up of Jews removed the bodies of their fellow inmates from the gas chambers, brought them to the crematoria, and then cleaned the gas chambers in preparation for the next victims.

Some victims died almost immediately, while others lingered for twenty minutes at most. After about thirty minutes ventilation fans were turned on and the chambers opened. The corpses then had to be removed from the gas chambers, another task that fell to the *Sonderkommandos*. After all gold teeth were removed from the victims and the women's hair cut off, the *Sonderkommandos* took the bodies to the ovens of the crematoria for burning. They also had to clean the gas chambers in preparation for the next load of victims. The *Sonderkommandos*, often numbering in the hundreds, were looked upon by other Jews as traitors for working for the Nazis, even though their labor was anything but voluntary. So closely involved with the killing process, the *Sonderkommandos* gained knowledge of the crimes being committed by the Nazis. Most of them were killed by the SS after two to four months of working in the crematoria. They were replaced by a new group freshly arrived from the trains, who worked until they, too, were eliminated.

A Dreadful Tally

The Nazis designed the Holocaust killing centers to streamline the process of mass murder with industrial assembly line efficiency. Considering the number of victims who died there, they succeeded. From the first deaths at Chelmno in December 1941 to the liberation of the camps in 1944 and 1945, almost 3 million Jews perished in the six killing centers. At Chelmno 152,000 died, while at the three Operation Reinhard camps, more than 1.5 million innocent victims were gassed or shot. Auschwitz-Birkenau recorded the most victims of any single camp, with 1.1 million deaths. Majdanek was the scene of at least 95,000 killings.

The Holocaust killing centers were the embodiment of Adolf Hitler's "Final Solution to the Jewish Question." Neither before nor since has any nation conducted such a systematic program of mass murder. Although the Nazis succeeded in destroying millions of lives, their effort ultimately failed: The Jewish population had been decimated but not eliminated. That fact would become an unintended legacy of the Third Reich.

CHAPTER FIVE

Resistance, Escape, and Liberation

Within the barbed wire fences of the Holocaust camps thousands of prisoners lived lives of desperate conformity, knowing that the slightest sign of opposition meant either torture or immediate death by an SS guard's bullet. There were, however, a few daring souls who risked everything to resist their Nazi oppressors. Attempts to obstruct a camp's well-organized routine were few and almost always doomed to failure. But the courage it took to mount even a small measure of resistance proved that the horrors of the concentration camps could not destroy the will to live.

Uprising at Treblinka

In 1942 the Nazis initiated *Aktion 1005* (Operation 1005), a plan to destroy all evidence of mass murder in the camps. Prisoners were forced to exhume buried corpses and incinerate them. Once a camp was cleared of evidence, the surviving prisoners were killed. When *Aktion 1005* began at Treblinka in 1943, the inmates knew that their end was near, so a small group decided to stage a revolt.

Prisoner Julian Chorazycki, former captain in the Polish army, set up a secret organizing committee with several fellow inmates to plan the rebellion. Their first job was to try to acquire weapons for their revolt from outside the camp. Chorazycki was able to obtain money from the camp's "gold Jews," prisoners who received and sorted gold, money, and other valuables taken from new arrivals to the camp. One day in April Chorazycki was caught by the camp's deputy commander while hiding a large amount of cash. After a brief struggle he managed to flee, but once outside, Chorazycki realized that escape was impossible. He committed suicide by drinking a vial of poison.

The loss of their leader did not stop the committee, which by now numbered some sixty prisoners. Inmate Marceli Galewski took over as committee leader and finalized the strategy for the revolt. According to the plan, the rebels would take over Treblinka, killing as many guards as possible, then set the camp on fire and escape. On August 2, 1943, the committee put its plan into action. Since the attempts to buy weapons had failed, the committee stole rifles, pistols, and hand grenades from the camp armory, distributing them among the rebels. After a guard confronted one of the members, the committee was forced to start the revolt early, before all the weapons had been taken. "At 3:45 p.m.," survivor Samuel Rajzman recalls, "we heard the signal—a rifleshot near the gates of the Jewish barracks. This shot was followed by the detonations of hand grenades. . . . An enormous fire broke out in the whole camp."[45]

Dark smoke filled the sky as a gasoline storage tank exploded. The rebels spread through the camp, killing several guards. Without enough weapons, many of the rebels were forced to fight with axes and pitchforks. Although caught by surprise, the guards soon returned fire. "From a nearby tower," writes survivor Shmuel (Samuel) Wilenberg, "a machine gun spit out bursts of fire. They hit their mark, thinning our ranks."[46] Eventually the rebellion was crushed by the superior firepower of the guards. About three hundred prisoners managed to escape the camp in the confusion. Most were recaptured and executed, but about one hundred escapees survived. Among the 350 to 400 prisoners killed in the revolt were Galewski and most of the committee members.

The *Sonderkommando* Revolt

Conditions at Auschwitz-Birkenau were so horrific that even prisoners who received special treatment from their Nazi captors could be pushed to revolt. The *Sonderkommandos* at Auschwitz-Birkenau enjoyed comfortable beds, better food, and the chance to shower at any time. These privileges were intended to keep them complacent and less likely to mount a rebellion. But in October 1944 workers in several of the camp's crematoria began just such a revolt.

Late in the war, the number of trains arriving at Auschwitz-Birkenau was dwindling. Rumors circulated that the gassing operations would soon come to an end and the remaining *Sonderkommandos* would be executed. A group of resistance leaders decided to try to preempt that event by staging a rebellion in the camp. This was not a new idea; preparations for an uprising had been going on for months. Several Jewish women working at a nearby munitions factory had been stealing small amounts of explosives and smuggling them into the camp. The resistance planned to use these explosives to destroy Birkenau's gas chambers and crematoria and then lead a general revolt of the inmates.

Around midday on October 7 the resistance received a warning that liquidation was imminent, so the *Sonderkommandos* put their plan into action. Carrying the smuggled explosives and stolen weapons, workers attacked the SS guards and set off detonations in Cre-

Modern-day students get a glimpse of what it was like to be crammed into a German train car used to transport Jews to Nazi death camps—and how difficult it was for those aboard the trains to escape. Remarkably, some prisoners managed to escape.

matorium IV. Miklos Nyiszli, the Jewish physician and Auschwitz prisoner who worked as a research pathologist for Josef Mengele, observed the *Sonderkommandos* "had taken possession of number one crematorium and, from every window and door, were spraying the SS troops with bullets and grenades."[47] Some reports tell of rebels throwing a German Kapo alive into a crematorium oven. It did not take long for the SS to regroup and counterattack, and the outcome was never in doubt, as Nyiszli recounts: "For about ten minutes the fighting was heavy on both sides. Loud machine gun fire from the watch towers mingled with the lesser blasts of the sub-machine guns, and interspersed could be heard the explosion of hand grenades and dynamite. Then, as suddenly as it had begun, everything became quiet."[48]

> "From a nearby tower a machine gun spit out bursts of fire. They hit their mark, thinning our ranks."[46]
>
> —Treblinka uprising survivor Shmuel (Samuel) Wilenberg.

The revolt cost the lives of 451 prisoners and 3 SS officers. Four Jewish women who had smuggled the explosives into Birkenau were arrested. On January 6, 1945, they were hanged in front of the remaining prisoners as a warning against further conspiracies. If any good came from the *Sonderkommando* rebellion, it was that Crematorium IV was so badly damaged, it could never again be used to burn the bodies of innocent people.

Escape from the Death Trains

The journey to the Holocaust camps usually meant death in the gas chambers for the deportees packed into the boxcars and cattle cars of the *Reichsbahn* trains. During the trip many contemplated escape before they reached their final destination. To most of the deportees the locked doors and Nazi guards created an insurmountable obstacle to freedom. But hundreds of brave captives risked everything to flee the death trains and vanish into the surrounding countryside.

Many of the cattle cars used to transport deportees had small windows blocked by barbed wire or metal bars. In one such car Leo Bretholz planned his escape. As the train rumbled toward Auschwitz, Bretholz and a friend struggled to loosen the window bars by using their pullovers as improvised ropes. To strengthen the grip on the bars, the men soaked their pullovers in the car's waste bucket. "I bent down and soaked my pullover in urine," Bretholz recalls. "I felt humiliated. It was the most disgusting thing I had ever done."[49] Finally successful, Bretholz and his friend jumped as the train rounded a corner, escaping into the night.

On another train bound for Auschwitz, several men managed to break open the boxcar door. Eleven-year-old Simon Gronowski was riding in the car with his mother. "My mother held me by my shirt and my shoulders. But at first, I did not dare to jump because the train was going too fast," Simon recalls. "But then at a certain moment, I felt the train slow down. I told my mother: 'Now I can jump.' She let me go and I jumped off."[50] Simon fled to the nearby forest and eventually found his father in Brussels, Belgium. They spent the rest of the war hiding, separately, with Catholic families in Belgium.

> "But then at a certain moment, I felt the train slow down. I told my mother: 'Now I can jump.' She let me go and I jumped off."[50]
>
> —Holocaust survivor Simon Gronowski.

A 2014 study by historian Tanja von Fransecky reveals that 764 Jews escaped from the Holocaust trains. "I was amazed that this happened at all," von Fransecky says, noting that many escapees felt remorse at leaving loved ones behind. "It is one of the reasons why many survivors kept silent for years after the war."[51]

Driving Out of Auschwitz

Most escapes from concentration camps were made quickly and quietly: slipping under the fence at night or breaking away from a work detail outside the camp. But one inmate of Auschwitz chose to boldly escape by driving through the camp's main gate.

Kazimierz Piechowski was a nineteen-year-old boy scout in Poland when the Nazis captured him and sent him to Auschwitz. When he learned that fellow prisoner Eugeniusz Bendera was to be executed soon, Piechowski planned an escape. On June 20, 1942, Piechowski and two other prisoners, Józef Lempart and Stanislaw Jaster, broke into a storeroom and donned SS uniforms. Bendera, a mechanic who maintained the camp's vehicles, sneaked into the garage and stole a fast and powerful Steyr 220—the camp commandant's car. After

Operation Harvest Festival

Despite its deceptively innocent title, *Aktion Erntefest* (Operation Harvest Festival) was the greatest single slaughter of Jews by the Germans during World War II. Alarmed by the uprisings at Sobibor and Treblinka, Nazi leaders resolved to prevent further resistance by killing all of the remaining Jews in Lublin, a district in the General Government region.

Preparations for the massacre began in October, 1943, when Jews in three camps—Majdanek, Trawniki, and Poniatowa—were told to dig long, zig-zag ditches supposedly to protect the camps against attack. In reality, the Jews were digging their own mass graves. At the morning roll call on November 3, Jewish prisoners at Majdanek were separated from the other inmates. According to Soviet records, "The shootings started early in the morning and ceased late in the evening. The SS brought the people, stripped naked, to the ditches in groups of fifty or one hundred. They were packed into the bottom of the ditch face down and shot with automatic rifles. Then a new group of people was piled on the corpses and shot in the same manner; and so on until the pits were full."

The same scene was played out at Trawniki and Poniatowa. To obscure the sounds of the shots and screams of the victims, music blared from loudspeakers placed near the trenches. By the end of the two-day Operation Harvest Festival, forty-three thousand Jews had been murdered.

Quoted in Nizkor Project. www.nizkor.org.

Bendera also put on a uniform, the four piled into the car and headed for the main gate, which was manned by SS guards.

"We are driving towards the final barrier," recalls Piechowski, "but it is closed. . . . We have 80 meters to go, it is still closed."[52] Finally, they stopped less than 100 feet (30.5 m) from the gate, unsure of what to do next. Piechowski started to get out when the guards noticed that the car's occupants wore SS officer uniforms. The guards quickly opened the barrier and the Steyr barreled through. The four had escaped without a shot being fired.

After hours of driving, the car broke down and the escapees continued on foot, ultimately eluding capture and surviving the war. In retaliation for the escape, the Nazis imprisoned Jaster's parents in Auschwitz, where they perished. Although Piechowski had daringly escaped Auschwitz, the horrors of the camp stayed with him for decades in anguished nightmares. Still, he remains true to his responsibility as a boy scout. "I am a scout," he states proudly, "so I have to do my duty—and be cheerful and merry. And I will be a scout to the end of my life."[53]

Breakout at Sobibor

Thoughts of escape were sometimes all that kept prisoners from losing their sanity. Although military experience was helpful in planning an escape, such expertise was hard to find in the brutal environs of the camps. At Sobibor, one man had such experience, and it was put to good use.

Soviet prisoner of war Alexander Pechersky had only recently come to Sobibor, but his defiant attitude toward the guards won the admiration of the other prisoners. Pechersky was approached by Leon Feldhendler, a prisoner representing a group of Polish Jews. "We had thought about [escaping] more than once," Feldhendler said, "but we didn't know how. You are a Soviet man, a military man. Tell us what to do and we'll do it."[54] Forming an underground committee of Soviet and Polish prisoners, the men came up with an escape plan: They would dig a tunnel under the fence so that all the prisoners could run to freedom in the nearby forest.

The group began digging the tunnel at night, but it was soon flooded by heavy rains. They needed a new plan. Since the inmates outnumbered their captors, killing the SS guards and then simply walking out of the camp at evening roll call seemed a workable option. The rebels would lure the guards to workshops on the pretext of inspecting work, then kill them quietly so as not to arouse suspicion.

After postponing the plan for one day, on October 14, 1943, the underground began asking the guards to come to various shops at fifteen- to thirty-minute intervals. The first guard was killed at about

3:30 p.m., followed by others dispatched quietly with axes or knives. The prisoners armed themselves with the guards' pistols as well as other weapons confiscated from the camp armory. In all, eleven SS men, including the camp commandant, were killed. All was going

Successful escape attempts from the camps were rare. In one such attempt in 1942, four Auschwitz prisoners donned SS uniforms (similar to those pictured), stole a camp official's car, and drove out the main gate. The four miraculously eluded capture and survived the war.

Eisenhower Surveys a Holocaust Camp

General Dwight D. Eisenhower was a career soldier who commanded the D-Day invasion of Normandy on June 6, 1944. As a hardened veteran, he had seen the worst of war on the battlefield. But after a visit to Ohrdruf, a subcamp of Buchenwald, Eisenhower knew that the world must be told about the horrors of the Holocaust. In a letter to General George C. Marshall, Eisenhower writes,

I have never felt able to describe my emotional reactions when I first came face to face with indisputable evidence of Nazi brutality and ruthless disregard of every shred of decency. Up to that time I had known about it only generally or through secondary sources. I am certain, however, that I have never at any other time experienced an equal sense of shock.

I visited every nook and cranny of the camp because I felt it my duty to be in a position from then on to testify at first hand about these things in case there ever grew up at home the belief or assumption that "the stories of Nazi brutality were just propaganda." Some members of the visiting party were not able to go through the ordeal. I not only did so but . . . I sent communications to both Washington and London, urging the two governments to send instantly to Germany a random group of newspaper editors. . . . I felt that the evidence should be immediately placed before the American and British publics in a fashion that would leave no room for cynical doubt.

Dwight D. Eisenhower, *Crusade in Europe*. Garden City, NY: Doubleday, 1949, pp. 408–409.

according to plan until one guard failed to show up for his scheduled appointment, and another was killed in a garage, where his body was likely to be discovered.

Pechersky decided to stage the roll call earlier than planned. The organized escape envisioned by the underground descended into disorder and panic. The remaining guards opened fire as the prisoners rushed toward the gate and the fences. "Suddenly we heard shots," recalls survivor Ada Lichtman. "In the beginning only a few shots, then it turned into heavy shooting, including machine-gun fire. . . . Riot and confusion prevailed, everything was thundering around."[55] Of the six hundred prisoners in the camp about three hundred managed to escape. One hundred of these were caught and executed; despite an extensive search, the rest eluded capture and made their way to freedom.

Death March from Auschwitz

By late 1944 Allied troops were pushing relentlessly toward the camps, leaving the Nazis no time to murder and cremate the thousands of inmates that remained. Their last hope was to lead the prisoners away from the conquering armies. As exhausted prisoners fell by the wayside, these forced evacuations turned into death marches.

When Soviet troops advanced through Poland in November 1944 the SS administration at Auschwitz began to destroy evidence of the camp. They ordered prisoners to demolish the crematoria and other buildings. But the most obvious proof of Nazi atrocities was the prisoners themselves, who could tell their stories to the liberating armies. In January 1945 about sixty-six thousand mostly Jewish prisoners began a forced march out of Auschwitz toward other camps in the interior of Germany. Dressed in their thin prison uniforms, the prisoners were at the mercy of the harsh winter weather. About fifteen thousand prisoners perished during the Auschwitz death march. Nine-year-old Thomas Buergenthal, one of many children who were forced to march with the adults, years later recalled the experience:

> They came in to announce that the camp was being liquidated. They gave us some food, and began to march us out of the camp. . . . After about a 10 to 12 hour walk we began to be very

tired. The children began to fall back. People from the back were pushing, that we weren't going fast enough. And whoever sat down was shot by guards at each side of the road.[56]

In late January 1945 some seven thousand prisoners, mostly women, were forced to endure a ten-day march from Stutthof concentration camp and its satellite camps near Danzig, Poland, toward the Baltic Sea. Upon reaching the shore the women were forced to enter the water where they were machine-gunned to death. Only thirteen prisoners survived. Beginning in March the Nazis forced about 30,000 prisoners of Buchenwald on a death march to prevent their rescue by US troops. About 8,000 people died along the route. On April 26, SS guards at Dachau began a six-day march of some seven thousand inmates. Those who survived the march were rescued by American troops in May.

There were nearly sixty death marches from Holocaust camps during the final months of World War II, resulting in between 200,000 and 250,000 deaths. All were made under the same conditions: prisoners forced to walk with little or no food or rest, prodded on by sadistic guards who killed any stragglers. The ill or injured prisoners left behind in the camps could only wait for death or rescue.

Liberation

In December 1944 the Nazis launched their final attempt to turn the tide of war in their favor. The Battle of the Bulge in the Ardennes forest of France and Belgium was the final defeat for the Third Reich. As Allied troops headed toward Germany from the west, the Soviet Red Army was advancing from the east. Caught in the middle, the Germans did their best to destroy the evidence of their atrocities. They did not succeed.

By this time some camps were already closed. The Operation Reinhard camps—Belzec, Sobibor, and Treblinka—were dismantled in 1943, the evidence of their existence disguised by farms built on the camps' sites. Majdanek was the first Holocaust camp to be liberated by the Allied forces. On July 23, 1944, soldiers of the Soviet Red Army entered Majdanek, encountering around five hundred survivors. The Nazis had partially burned the camp in a hurried evacuation, but the crematorium stood as grim confirmation of the atrocities that had

Upon entering Buchenwald concentration camp in April 1945, US soldiers encounter a trailer piled high with naked human corpses. Allied soldiers who liberated the camps discovered thousands of decaying bodies. They also found survivors; some were barely alive but others rejoiced.

taken place there. Through photographs and news reports, the world got its first look at what previously had been only rumors of Nazi brutality. In the first published eyewitness account of the camps, Soviet journalist Roman Karmen writes,

> It is difficult to believe it myself but my eyes cannot deceive me. I see the human bones, lime barrels, chlorine pipes and furnace machinery. I see the enormous dumps of shoes, sandals and slippers in men's, women's and children's sizes bearing the trademarks of a dozen European countries. . . . The Russian Army came in time to save the last set of victims earmarked for slaughter.[57]

The survivors, looking like living skeletons, embraced the liberating troops tentatively, as if they dared not believe their rescue was actually happening. Survivor Viktor Frankl recalls, "Timidly, we looked around and glanced at each other questioningly. Then we ventured a few steps out of the camp. This time no orders were shouted at us, nor was there any need to duck quickly to avoid a blow or a kick."[58]

The advance of the Allies progressed quickly, and on May 8, 1945, Germany officially surrendered. By the middle of May, Mauthausen, Dachau, Dora-Mittelbau, Ravensbrück, and the other camps had been liberated. For the surviving victims of the Holocaust, the war was finally over. Allied soldiers who walked through the camps were shocked to see stacks of decaying corpses. They forced civilian members of the Nazi Party to dig new graves and bury the dead. In many camps the liberators led local German citizens past the gas chambers, crematoria, and mass graves, to see evidence of what their countrymen had done in the name of Hitler's Final Solution.

> "It is difficult to believe it myself but my eyes cannot deceive me. I see the human bones, lime barrels, chlorine pipes and furnace machinery."[57]
>
> —Soviet journalist Roman Karmen.

More than seven hundred thousand survivors were left behind at the camps, among them thousands too ill or malnourished to be saved. Those who survived mourned the loss of their homes, families, and friends. Many became displaced persons, with nowhere to go and no one to take care of them. Because of the Holocaust, the population of European Jews fell from 9.5 million in 1933 to about 3.5 million in 1950.

"Never Forget"

Most of the Holocaust camps are gone today, destroyed by the Nazis or the ravages of time. Of those that remain, some have been turned into museums or memorials. Visitors freely walk the same ground where victims of hatred once were forced to run to their deaths. The gas chambers are just empty rooms now, the ovens cold and silent. At the memorial site of the Treblinka camp is a stone marker bearing a message in six languages. In Hebrew, French, English, German, Polish, and Greek, are the words "Never Forget." It is a plea from the ghosts of 11 million victims that, by remembering them, a tragedy like the Holocaust will never happen again.

SOURCE NOTES

Introduction: The Camps of the Third Reich

1. Quoted in Birkbeck University of London, "*Münchener Neueste Nachrichten: Report on the Opening of the Dachau Concentration Camp, 21 March, 1933*." www.camps.bbk.ac.uk.

2. Quoted in Jewish Virtual Library, "Adolf Hitler: Threats Against the Jews." www.jewishvirtuallibrary.org.

Chapter One: Journey to Extinction

3. Quoted in Abraham I. Katsch, trans. and ed., *Scroll of Agony: The Warsaw Diary of Chaim A. Kaplan*. New York: Macmillan, 1965, p. 19.

4. Quoted in Lucy S. Dawidowicz, ed., *A Holocaust Reader*. Springfield, NJ: Behrman House, 1976, pp. 59, 60.

5. Quoted in Aktion Reinhard Camps, "Piotrkow Trybunalski Ghetto." www.deathcamps.org.

6. Quoted in Willy Georg and Rafael F. Scharf, *In the Warsaw Ghetto Summer 1941*. New York: Aperture Foundation, 1993, p. 108.

7. Primo Levi, *Survival in Auschwitz: If This Is a Man*. New York: Orion, 1959, p. 12.

8. Quoted in Aktion Reinhard Camps, "The Gerstein Report." www.deathcamps.org.

9. Rena Kornreich Gelissen, *Rena's Promise: A Story of Sisters in Auschwitz*. Boston: Beacon, 1995, p. 51.

10. Gelissen, *Rena's Promise*, p. 52.

11. Quoted in Yitzhak Arad, *Belzec, Sobibor, Treblinka: The Operation Reinhard Death Camps*. Bloomington: Indiana University Press, 1987, p. 63.

12. Quoted in Tamara L. Roleff, ed. *The Holocaust: Death Camps*. San Diego: Greenhaven, 2002, p. 44.

13. Quoted in Arad, *Belzec, Sobibor, Treblinka*, p. 84.

Chapter Two: Slaves of the Reich

14. Yale Law School, "Wannsee Protocol, January 20, 1942," Avalon Project. http://avalon.law.yale.edu.

15. Quoted in Michael Thad Allen, *The Business of Genocide: The SS, Slave Labor, and the Concentration Camps*. Chapel Hill: University of North Carolina, 2002, p. 43.

16. Quoted in Martin Gilbert, *The Holocaust: A History of the Jews of Europe During the Second World War*. New York: Holt, Reinhart and Winston, 1985, p. 57.

17. Quoted in Michael W. Perry, ed., *Dachau Liberated: The Official Report by the US Seventh Army Released Within Days of the Camp's Liberation by Elements of the 42nd and 45th Divisions*. Seattle: Inkling, 2000, pp. 48–49.

18. Levi, *Survival in Auschwitz*, p. 69.

19. Quoted in Sara Tuvel Bernstein, *The Seamstress: A Memoir of Survival*. New York: Berkley, 1997, p. 200.

20. Quoted in Bernstein, *The Seamstress*, p. 200.

21. Bernstein, *The Seamstress*, pp. 210, 211.

22. Felix Landau, *No Longer Alone: My Intimate Walk with Jesus Christ*. Bloomington, IN: West Bow, 2011, p. 30.

Chapter Three: Human Guinea Pigs

23. Siegfried Knapp and Ted Brusaw, *Soldat: Reflections of a German Soldier, 1936–1949*. New York: Orion, 1992, p. 202.

24. Quoted in Harvard Law School Library, Nuremburg Trials Project: A Digital Document Collection, p. 168. http://nuremberg.law.harvard.edu.

25. Quoted in Harvard Law School Library, Nuremburg Trials Project, p. 178.

26. Quoted in Konnilyn G. Feig, *Hitler's Death Camps: The Sanity of Madness*. New York: Holmes & Meier, 1979, p. 56.

27. Quoted in Vivien Spitz, *Doctors from Hell: The Horrific Account of Nazi Experiments on Humans*. Boulder, CO: Sentient, 2005, p. 107.

28. Quoted in Spitz, *Doctors from Hell*, p. 107.

29. Quoted in Naomi Baumslag, *Murderous Medicine: Nazi Doctors, Human Experimentation, and Typhus*. Westport, CT: Praeger, 2005, p. 143.

30. Quoted in Feig, *Hitler's Death Camps*, p. 146.

31. Quoted in Robert Jay Lifton, *The Nazi Doctors: Medical Killing and the Psychology of Genocide*. New York: Basic, 1986, p. 345.

32. Quoted in Lifton, *The Nazi Doctors*, p. 348.

33. Miklos Nyiszli, Tibère Kramer, and Richard Seaver, trans., *Auschwitz: A Doctor's Eyewitness Account*. New York: Arcade, 2011, p. 58.

Chapter Four: The Killing Grounds

34. Quoted in Mario R. Dederichs, *Heydrich: The Face of Evil*. Drexel Hill, PA: Casemate, 2009, p.16.

35. Quoted in Robert Gerwarth, *Hitler's Hangman: The Life of Heydrich*. New Haven, CT: Yale University, 2011, p. 286.

36. Quoted in Ernst Klee, Willi Dressen, and Volker Riess, eds., *The Good Old Days: The Holocaust as Seen by Its Perpetrators and Bystanders*. Old Saybrook, CT: Konecky & Konecky, 1991, p. 218.

37. Quoted in Jewish Virtual Library, "Belzec: Testimony from a Camp Engineer." www.jewishvirtuallibrary.org.

38. Quoted in Arad, *Belzec, Sobibor, Treblinka*, p. 24.

39. Quoted in Arad, *Belzec, Sobibor, Treblinka*, p. 83.

40. Quoted in Arad, *Belzec, Sobibor, Treblinka*, p. 24.

41. Quoted in Arad, *Belzec, Sobibor, Treblinka*, p. 86.

42. Levi, *Survival in Auschwitz*, p. 14.

43. Shlomo Venezia, *Inside the Gas Chambers: Eight Months in the Sonderkommando of Auschwitz*. Malden, MA: Polity, 2009, p. 77.

44. Quoted in Eugene Aroneanu, comp., and Thomas Whissen, trans., *Inside the Concentration Camps: Eyewitness Accounts of Life in Hitler's Death Camps*. Westport, CT: Praeger, 1996, p. 128.

Chapter Five: Resistance, Escape, and Liberation

45. Samuel Rajzman, "Uprising in Treblinka," Holocaust History Project. www.holocaust-history.org.

46. Quoted in Arad, *Belzec, Sobibor, Treblinka*, p. 292.

47. Nyiszli, Kramer, and Seaver, *Auschwitz: A Doctor's Eyewitness Account*, p. 158.

48. Nyiszli, Kramer, and Seaver, *Auschwitz: A Doctor's Eyewitness Account*, p. 159.

49. Quoted in Tony Paterson, "The Leaps of Faith That Saved a Brave Few from Auschwitz's Horrors: New Study Reveals How Hundreds of Jews Used Desperate Means to Jump from Nazi Trains," *Independent* (UK), April 8, 2014. www.independent.co.uk.

50. Quoted in Althea Williams and Sarah Erlich, "Escaping the Train to Auschwitz," BBC News, April 19, 2013. www.bbc.com.

51. Quoted in *Forward* Staff, "How 764 Jews Jumped from Shoah Trains to Escape Death Camps," *Jewish Daily Forward*, April 9, 2014. www.forward.com.

52. Quoted in Homa Khaleeli, "I Escaped from Auschwitz," *Guardian*, April 11, 2011. www.theguardian.com.

53. Quoted in Khaleeli, "I Escaped from Auschwitz."

54. Quoted in Arad, *Belzec, Sobibor, Treblinka*, p. 309.

55. Quoted in Arad, *Belzec, Sobibor, Treblinka*, p. 331.

56. Quoted in Michael Berenbaum, *The World Must Know: The History of the Holocaust as Told in the United States Holocaust Memorial Museum*. Boston: Little, Brown, 1993, pp. 182–83.

57. Quoted in *Time*, "Poland: Vernichtungslager," August 24, 1944. http://time.com.

58. Quoted in United States Holocaust Memorial Museum, "Liberation." www.ushmm.org.

Adolf Eichmann

As head of the Gestapo's Department of Jewish Affairs, Eichmann coordinated the transportation of Jews from the ghettos to the Holocaust camps.

Hans Frank

Governor-General of the Nazi-occupied territory in Poland, Frank oversaw the deportation and imprisoning of Jews in the ghettos. Although four killing centers were constructed during his administration, he claimed no knowledge of them.

Reinhard Heydrich

The leading architect of the "Final Solution," Heydrich created the ruthless *Einsatzgruppen*, or mobile death squads. After his assassination in 1942 the first killing centers were created in an operation named in his honor.

Heinrich Himmler

The leader (*Reichsführer)* of the SS, Himmler was the second most powerful man in Nazi Germany. He was appointed by Hitler to create the Nazi system of concentration camps.

Adolf Hitler

Founder of the National Socialist German Workers' (Nazi) Party and chancellor of Germany from 1933 to 1945. An anti-Semite, his plan to create an Aryan "Master Race" led to the Holocaust and the extermination of 6 million Jews.

Rudolf Höss

The commandant of Auschwitz, Höss presided over the deaths of approximately 1.1 million prisoners.

Primo Levi

A Jewish chemist imprisoned in Auschwitz-Birkenau in 1944, Levi survived the Holocaust and wrote of his experiences in the camp.

Josef Mengele

A doctor known as the Angel of Death, Mengele performed gruesome medical procedures on prisoners at Auschwitz. His fanatical interest in genetics led him to experiment on twin children.

Miklos Nyiszli

A doctor and prisoner at Auschwitz who assisted Josef Mengele in his experiments. Nyiszli's later writings detail the atrocities performed on unwilling inmates.

Alexander Pechersky

Soviet prisoner of war who masterminded the inmate uprising at Sobibor. The revolt was in part responsible for the Nazi "Harvest Festival" massacre.

Sigmund Rascher

Nazi physician who performed cruel high-altitude and freezing experiments to discover ways of increasing the survival rate of *Luftwaffe* pilots and Nazi soldiers on the Russian Front.

Books

Yitzhak Arad, *Belzec, Sobibor, Treblinka: The Operation Reinhard Death Camps*. Bloomington: Indiana University, 1999.

Eugene Aroneanu, comp., and Thomas Whissen, trans., *Inside the Concentration Camps: Eyewitness Accounts of Life in Hitler's Death Camps*. Westport, CT: Praeger, 1996.

David M. Crowe, *The Holocaust: Roots, History, and Aftermath*. Boulder, CO: Westview, 2008.

Jack R. Fischel, *Historical Dictionary of the Holocaust*. Lanham, MD: Scarecrow, 2010.

Yisrael Gutman and Michael Berenbaum, eds., *Anatomy of the Auschwitz Death Camp*. Bloomington: Indiana University, 2013.

David J. Hogan, Editor-in-Chief, *The Holocaust Chronicle*. Lincolnwood, IL: Publications International, 2003.

Eva Mozes Kor and Lisa Rojany Buccieri, *Surviving the Angel of Death: The Story of a Mengele Twin in Auschwitz*. Terre Haute, IN: Tanglewood, 2009.

Hal Marcovitz, *Life in Nazi Germany*. San Diego: ReferencePoint, 2015.

Don Nardo, *Life in a Nazi Concentration Camp*. San Diego: ReferencePoint, 2014.

Eve Nussbaum Soumerai and Carol D. Schulz, *Daily Life During the Holocaust*. Westport, CT: Greenwood, 2009.

Angela Gluck Wood, *Holocaust: The Events and Their Impact on Real People*. New York: DK, 2007.

Internet Sources

Dr. X., "Concentration Camp," *Atlantic*. www.theatlantic.com/maga zine/archive/1939/09/concentration-camp/308926/?single_page =true.

Rochelle G. Saidel, "Ravensbrück Women's Concentration Camp," Jewish Women's Archive. http://jwa.org/encyclopedia/article/ravens bruck-womens-concentration-camp.

Science Daily, "Survivor of Nazi 'Twin Experiments' Talks to Doctors About Human Subjects Research." www.sciencedaily.com/releases /2012/12/121206153357.htm.

US Holocaust Memorial Museum, "Children During the Holocaust." www.ushmm.org/wlc/en/article.php?ModuleId=10005142.

Websites

The Holocaust Explained (www.theholocaustexplained.org). Features Holocaust studies keyed to students eleven to sixteen years old.

The Holocaust History Project (www.holocaust-history.org). An archive of informational essays, videos, documents, and photographs about the Holocaust. Includes a special section refuting those who deny that the Holocaust ever happened.

Jewish Virtual Library (www.jewishvirtuallibrary.org/jsource/holo .html). The Holocaust page of this website contains information about all aspects of the Holocaust.

US Holocaust Memorial Museum (www.ushmm.org). A comprehensive guide to the Holocaust, including articles, photographs, films, survivor accounts, and information about the museum in Washington, DC.

Yad Vashem (www.yadvashem.org). The website of the official Jewish Holocaust memorial. Presents articles, photographs, a database of victims' names, and an online document catalog.

INDEX